POP QUIZ?

How much do you know about TV's hippest Vampire Slayer? Think you know every episode by heart? Maybe you've seen them all—but that doesn't necessarily mean that you're up to par on your Buffy trivia. Test your knowledge on these *killer* questions:

- What was Buffy's grade point average when entering Sunnydale High?
- Why does Giles hate computers?
- What is unusual about Willow's bedroom?

Packed with tons of trivia, a special photo insert, and quizzes to test your knowledge of the anti-fang gang. Find all these answers and more in . . .

Pop Quiz: Buffy the Vampire Slayer

Buffy the Vampire Slayer™

Buffy the Vampire Slayer (movie tie-in)
The Harvest
Halloween Rain
Coyote Moon
Night of the Living Rerun
The Angel Chronicles, Vol. 1
Blooded
The Angel Chronicles, Vol. 2
The Xander Years, Vol. 1
Visitors
Unnatural Selection
The Angel Chronicles, Vol. 3
The Power of Persuasion
The Willow Files, Vol. 1

Available from ARCHWAY Paperbacks

Buffy the Vampire Slayer adult books

Child of the Hunt
Return to Chaos
The Gatekeeper Trilogy
    Book 1: Out of the Madhouse
    Book 2: Ghost Roads
    Book 3: Sons of Entropy
Obsidian Fate
Immortal
Sins of the Father

The Watcher's Guide: The Official Companion to the Hit Show
The Postcards
The Essential Angel
The Sunnydale High Yearbook
Pop Quiz: Buffy the Vampire Slayer

Available from POCKET BOOKS

BUFFY
THE VAMPIRE
SLAYER™

POP QUIZ

Cynthia Boris

POCKET PULSE

New York   London   Toronto   Sydney   Singapore

An *Original* Publication of POCKET BOOKS

 POCKET PULSE, published by
Pocket Books, a division of Simon & Schuster Inc.
1230 Avenue of the Americas, New York, NY 10020

ISBN: 0-671-04258-0

First Pocket Books printing December 1999

10 9 8 7 6 5 4 3 2 1

POCKET PULSE and colophon are trademarks of Simon & Schuster Inc.

Printed in the U.S.A.

Dedications are always tough to write, since so many people are involved in the making of any book. Obviously, we wouldn't even be here if it wasn't for Joss Whedon and the wonderfully talented cast and crew of *Buffy*. My thanks to them, and especially to the writers who gave me so many great lines to work with. Personally, I have to thank the girls at JYGML, including Becky, Karen, Meer, Miriam, and Elaine, and also Jeanne Gold, all of whom acted as guinea pigs while I tried to create harder and harder trivia. Among them all, they couldn't be stumped.

Contents

Class, close your books, clear your desks, and sharpen a #2 pencil. It's time for a pop quiz. Have no fear—it's not English, math, or history, it's Buffy the Vampire Slayer! Don't bother to keep your eyes on your own paper—in fact, it's more fun if you share. See if you have what it takes to be a super Slayer. Earn one point for every correct answer, then check the Slay-O-Meter to see where you fall. You could be the next protector of Sunnydale, a venerable Watcher, or an assistant Slayerette.

POP QUIZ

1

In the Beginning

Dig a bit into the history of this place and you'll find there've been a steady stream of fairly odd occurrences. I believe this area is the center of mystical energy. Things gravitate toward it that you might not find elsewhere.

—Giles on Sunnydale
"Welcome to the Hellmouth"

How much do you know about the town they built upon the Hellmouth? Dig deep into its history and you'll find more than just the dead underground. . . .

1. Sunnydale is in what state (1 in 50 shot here, folks)?

2. If you were a teen in Sunnydale, where would you hang out?

3. Name the park where the vampires troll.

1

4. Drive two hours by freeway and you can reach what department store? Macy's

5. If you'd rather have coffee and donuts, where would you go?

6. Sunnydale's main street has a few other shops. What are they?

7. There is a gumball machine in front of the magic shop that is oddly appropriate. Why?

8. Who is the mayor of Sunnydale? Wilkins

9. How many Starbucks can be found in Sunnydale?

10. Where is the ice cream bar?

11. In what year did the town have an earthquake that buried part of the city?

12. How many cemeteries are there within the city limits?

13. How many churches does Sunnydale have?

14. What happened to Principal Flutie? Eaten

15. What happened to Principal Snyder? Eaten

16. What are Sunnydale High's school colors?

17. What is the school mascot? Pig

18. He was in the background of dozens of episodes, from the pilot to the finale. Name this Sunnydale geek who tends to blend. Andrew

19. According to Buffy, how are vampires made?

20. Name the bartender who serves vampires and Slayers alike. _Willie_

21. Name the wooded area just outside of town.

22. And an easy one to help you catch your breath: Sunnydale is located on top of what? _Hellmouth_

23. The good part of town is how far from the bad part of town? _1 block_

24. What two sites are popular field trip destinations?

25. The Master has a real name. What is it?

Answers to the In the Beginning Quiz

1. California (southern, to be more exact)
2. The Bronze
3. Weatherly Park
4. Neiman Marcus
5. The Espresso Pump
6. Hardware store, magic shop, bookstore (Book Stew). Bonus points if you knew the name of the bookstore
7. The gum machine is shaped like a green monster
8. Mayor Richard Wilkins III
9. One

10. Past Hamilton Street

11. In 1937

12. 12, according to Giles in "Revelations"

13. 43

14. He was eaten by hyena-possessed students ("The Pack")

15. He was eaten by the mayor (Sensing a pattern here?)

16. Burgundy and gold

17. A razorback

18. Jonathan

19. "They have to suck your blood and then you have to suck their blood. It's a whole big sucking thing."

20. Willy the Snitch

21. Miller's Woods or Breaker's Woods

22. A Hellmouth

23. About half a block

24. The zoo and the Natural History Museum

25. Heinrich Joseph Nest

Slay-O-Meter for In the Beginning

0–10 Welcome to the Hellmouth. You have a lot of learning to do if you plan to survive.

11–19 You've almost got it. Spend a little less time hanging at the Bronze, study the more historical aspects of the town, and you'll be fine.

20–25 A native! Sounds like you were born and raised in Sunnydale. Is that a good thing?

2

Attendance

You're the Slayer and we're like, the Slayerettes!

—*Willow on joining Buffy in the hunt for witches*
"The Witch"

Even a great Slayer can't do it alone. Buffy has her Watcher and her friends to help her conquer the forces of darkness. See if you have what it takes to become an honorary Slayerette.

Buffy

    1. What is Buffy's last name? Summers.

    2. Name the woman who brought Buffy into this world. Joyce Summers

    3. Name the one scary guy who took her out of it (okay, only for a minute). Master

    4. What is Buffy's father's name? Hank Summers

5. Buffy's mother works in what kind of establishment? *Art Gallery*

6. What does Buffy's father do for a living?

7. Where did Buffy go to school before coming to Sunnydale? *Henly*

8. Why was she kicked out of her previous school? *Burnt Gym*

9. Who was Buffy's Watcher before Giles?

10. Buffy's middle name is a lot more common than her first. What is it? *Anne*

11. You see Buffy's house all the time, but what is her address?

12. As a child, Buffy wished she could be what ice skating champ?

13. What does Buffy like to sleep in?

14. What is the name of Buffy's stuffed pig?

15. According to vocational testing, Buffy should be in what field? *Correctional Officer*

Giles

1. What is Giles's first name?

2. Before coming to Sunnydale, Giles worked for what museum?

3. At what university did Giles study?

4. How old was Giles when he found out he was to be a Watcher?

5. What did Giles want to be when he grew up?

6. Giles has an abundance of what fabric in his wardrobe?

7. Two of Giles's relatives were also Watchers. Who were they?

8. Name Giles's one true love.

9. Name Giles's British buddy with a taste for sorcery.

10. Why does Giles hate computers?

11. What is Giles's idea of "fun"?

12. Giles has an oft-maligned car. What kind of car is it?

13. Giles is fluent in how many languages?

14. What are those languages?

15. What is hanging in the pass-through to Giles's kitchen?

Willow

1. What is Willow's last name?

2. Name Willow's mother.

3. Name Willow's father.

4. Willow and Xander first broke up when he did what unspeakable act?

5. Willow has a fear of what animal?

6. What kind of pet did Willow have?

7. What happened to her pet?

8. What instrument does Willow play?

9. What is unusual about Willow's bedroom?

10. According to vocational testing, what field should Willow go into?

Xander

1. What is Xander's full name, including his middle name?

2. How did Xander find out that Buffy is the Slayer?

3. What is the name of Xander's oft-mentioned uncle?

4. What is his mother's "famous" dinner?

5. What does Xander's father do for a living?

6. Xander has his own personal vehicle in the first season. What is it?

7. Xander's fear of clowns began at what age?

8. Trying to impress a girl, Xander did what disgusting act?

9. Xander has an unusual Christmas tradition. What is it?

10. According to vocational testing, what field should Xander go into?

Angel

1. What is Angel's historical name?
2. What does his historical name mean?
3. Angel has a tattoo on his back. What is it?
4. Name the country of Angel's birth.
5. Why is Angel able to resist feeding on humans?
6. What happened to Angel's parents?
7. Where was Buffy the first time Angel saw her?
8. How old is Angel (give or take a decade)?
9. Who sired Angel?
10. When did Angel come to America?

Cordelia

1. What is Cordelia's last name?
2. Who is Cordelia's favored "Cordette"?
3. Cordy has a personalized plate on her car. What does it say?
4. What is the significance of "Be my deputy"?
5. Cordy once took a job as what?
6. Cordy now labels things in life as happening "BX." What does that mean?
7. What color are Cordy's eyes?

8. According to Cordelia, there is one good reason for buying expensive items. Why?

9. How does Cordy take her cappuccino?

10. According to vocational testing, what field should Cordelia go into?

Oz

1. What is Oz's last name?

2. Oz drives what kind of vehicle?

3. What is Oz's "problem"?

4. Who else in Oz's family has this problem?

5. What is the name of Oz's band?

6. What is Oz's position in the band?

7. Name the band's lead singer.

8. Name all the colors Oz's hair has been dyed.

9. What color are his fingernails usually painted?

10. Oz has one ambition in life. What is it?

Answers to the Attendance Quiz

Buffy

1. Summers

2. Joyce Summers

3. The Master
4. Hank Summers
5. An art gallery
6. He is some kind of businessman
7. Hemerey High in Los Angeles
8. For burning down the gym, among other sins
9. Merrick
10. Anne
11. 1630 Revello Drive
12. Dorothy Hamill
13. A tank or camisole top and PJ bottoms
14. Mr. Gordo
15. Law enforcement

Giles

1. Rupert (is it a wonder they call him Giles?)
2. The British Museum (or, possibly, a British museum)
3. Oxford
4. Ten
5. A fighter pilot or a grocer
6. Tweed
7. His father and his father's mother
8. Jenny Calendar—recently departed

9. Ethan Rayne

10. Because they don't smell. He says the getting of knowledge should be "smelly."

11. At home with a cup of bovril and a good book.

12. A French (and very weary) Citroen

13. Five, and he is presumably passable in a dozen more

14. English, German, and Latin for sure. The other two haven't been mentioned.

15. A crystal

Willow

1. Rosenberg

2. Sheila Rosenberg

3. Ira Rosenberg

4. He stole her Barbie doll when they were little

5. Frogs

6. Fish

7. Angelus strung them on a thread and put them in an envelope

8. Piano, only not in front of people

9. It has French doors instead of windows

10. She is never told, since she is being wooed by a software conglomerate

Xander

1. Alexander Lavelle Harris (you only get the points if you knew Xander was short for Alexander)

2. He was up in the stacks of the library and heard Buffy and Giles talking

3. Uncle Roary

4. Her famous "phone call for Chinese"

5. Nothing—he appears to be unemployed

6. A skateboard

7. Six, thanks to a clown at his birthday party

8. He drank an entire gallon of Gatorade without taking a breath (after that there was an ick factor)

9. He sleeps in the backyard

10. The field of corrections (as in prison guard)

Angel

1. Angelus

2. "The one with the angelic face"

3. A winged lion

4. Ireland

5. Because he killed a gypsy girl

6. He killed them
7. Outside her old high school in LA
8. 246
9. Darla
10. About eighty years earlier

Cordelia

1. Chase
2. Harmony
3. Queen C
4. Cordy followed a forest ranger around on a school trip making a fool of herself
5. A salesgirl at a dress shop
6. Before Xander—as in, before they were dating
7. Hazel
8. Because they cost more
9. Cinnamon, chocolate, half-caff, nonfat, extra foam
10. A personal shopper or motivational speaker

Oz

1. We don't know
2. A van

3. He's a werewolf
4. His cousin Jordy
5. Dingos Ate My Baby
6. He plays guitar
7. Devon
8. Orange, black, blond
9. Black
10. E-flat, diminished 9th (a guitar chord)

Slay-O-Meter for Attendance

0–30 You must be new around here. Hang out at the Bronze, keep your ears open, and soon you'll be one of the gang.

31–60 You're in with the "in" crowd. Unfortunately, that means you hang with Cordelia. Better try harder.

61–80 You're in with the "out" crowd, and in Sunnydale, that's the safest place to be.

3

Knock, Knock; Who's There?

For I am Xander, king of all cretins, may all
lesser cretins bow before me.

—*Xander on opening his mouth*
"The Witch"

The only thing better than talking about yourself is talking about other people behind or
even in front of their backs. Name the "speaker" and the "speakee" in each quote. Give yourself an extra Slayer point if you know the
episode the quote comes from.

    1. "It's good to know you've seen the softer
side of Sears."
    2. "One of these days you have to get a
grown-up car."
    3. "Who died and made you Elvis?"

4. "I'd say he should get a girlfriend if he wasn't so old."

5. "She's lovely . . . in a common, extremely well-proportioned sort of way."

6. "You have a father's love for the child, and that is useless to the cause."

7. "Those boys aren't sparklingly normal as it is."

8. "He said he was going through all these changes. Then he went through all these . . . changes."

9. "I swear, one of these days you're going to wake up in a coma."

10. "Jimmy Olson jokes are pretty much gonna be lost on you."

11. "Princess Margaret here had a little trouble keeping up."

12. "The vampire kills you. We watch. We rejoice."

13. "I think you splashed on a little too much Obsession for Dorks."

14. "Check out Giles the next generation."

15. "He's usually Investigate Things from Every Boring Angle guy. Now he's I Cling to My One Lame Idea guy. What gives?"

16. "Someone wasn't worthy."

17. "You're Mister Test Scores!"

18. "She's not playing with a full deck. She has almost no deck. She has a three."

19. "Thank God, you're here. I was planning to panic."

20. "That's it. I'm puttin' a collar with a little bell on that guy."

21. "You need a personality. STAT."

22. "Can she cram complex issues into a nutshell or what?"

23. "Just because you were Guacamole Queen when you were three doesn't mean you understand how this works."

24. "Less together guy and more bad magic, hates the world, ticking time-bomb guy."

25. "Is he evil? The last one was evil."

Answers to the Knock, Knock; Who's There? Quiz

1. Cordelia to Willow—"Welcome to the Hellmouth"

2. Buffy to Giles—"Inca Mummy Girl"

3. Cordy to Xander on his sudden increase in sex appeal—"Bewitched, Bothered, and Bewildered"

4. Buffy on Giles—"The Witch"

5. Giles on Ms. French, the substitute teacher—"Teacher's Pet"

6. Travers on Giles's affection for Buffy—"Helpless"

7. Giles on Dave and Fritz—"I Robot, You Jane"

8. Willow on Oz's werewolf transformation—"Phases"

9. Cordy to Giles—"Gingerbread"

10. Xander on Giles's inability to understand pop culture references—"The Zeppo"

11. Faith on Wesley as he gasps for breath—"Doppelgangland"

12. Xander to Cordy as they hunt vampires in Buffy's absence—"Anne"

13. Cordy to Xander—"Phases"

14. Cordy on Wesley and his resemblance to Giles—"Consequences"

15. Xander on Giles's thought that Jenny is the ghost—"I Only Have Eyes for You"

16. Spike to Angel when Angel is unable to revive Acathla—"Becoming"

17. Willow to Oz on his inexplicable failure of senior year—"Anne"

18. Buffy on Faith's lack of sanity—"Faith, Hope and Trick"

19. Giles to Wesley on being captured by a demon (at this point he's abusing sarcasm)—"Bad Girls"

20. Xander on Angel's ability to appear and disappear so silently—"School Hard"

21. Buffy to Giles on his idea of fun—"Welcome to the Hellmouth"

22. Xander on Cordy, and he's being sarcastic—"Faith, Hope and Trick"

23. Cordy on Buffy's understanding of Homecoming—"Homecoming"

24. Buffy on Giles's teenage years—"Band Candy"

25. Buffy on Wesley and Mrs. Post—"Bad Girls"

Slay-O-Meter for Knock, Knock; Who's There?

0–15 "Spank your inner moppet, whatever, just get over it."

16–30 "We're right behind you! Only, a little further back."

31–50 "You're da man, Buff!"

4

Pop Goes the Culture

Pop culture reference, sorry.

—*Buffy to Giles*
"I Robot, You Jane"

The Sunnydale gang may not be English scholars, but they have Giles beat when it comes to pop culture. Name the cultural icon that is referred to in each of these quotes, and give yourself an extra point if you can name the episode it comes from.

1. "Maybe we should be looking for something like Slayer kryptonite."

2. "But gee, Mr. White, if Clark and Lois get all the big stories I'll never be a real reporter."

3. "If it weren't for you . . . Willow would be Robby the Robot's love slave."

4. "But shouldn't you be destroying the world right about now? Pulling the sword out of Al Franken, or whatever he's called?"

5. "If Giles wants to go after the fiend who murdered his girlfriend, I say Faster Pussycat Kill Kill."

6. "You're the Zeppo."

7. "So now we're Dr. Laura for the deceased."

8. "Thank you, Thighmaster."

9. "If he [death] asks you to play chess, don't even do it. Guy's like a whiz."

10. "If I see a floating pipe and a smoking jacket, he's dropped."

11. "In other words . . . 'This was no boating accident.' "

12. "If I can suggest . . . 'This time it's personal?' I mean, there's a reason why it's a classic."

13. "We're gonna need a bigger boat."

14. "You got the wrong *casa*, Mr. Belvedere."

15. "Man, this sucker wobbles but he won't fall down."

16. "I ran a statistical analysis and Hello Darkness—makes DC look like Mayberry."

17. "Call me Snyder. Just a last name—like Barbarino."

18. "If you don't mind a little Gene and Roger, I would leave off the idiot part."

19. "You were my sire, man. You were my Yoda!"

20. "Back off, Pink Ranger."

21. "You look like DeBarge!"

22. "Red Rum! Red Rum!"

23. "Does anybody else feel like we've been Keyser Soze'd?"

24. "I had the strangest dream, and you were in it, and you and you . . ."

25. "At least now you don't have to eat your Soylent Green."

Answers to the Pop Goes the Culture Quiz

1. Superman can be killed or disabled with kryptonite—"Helpless"

2. Superman again! (Clark Kent and Lois Lane)—"The Zeppo"

3. Robby was the famous robot from *Forbidden Planet*—"Phases"

4. Al Franken was a comedian on *Saturday Night Live*—"Becoming"

5. *Faster Pussycat! Kill! Kill!* was the title of a cult classic movie by Russ Meyer—"Passion"

6. Zeppo was the Marx Brothers' straight man, who is pretty much ignored in the history of this famous comedy team—"The Zeppo"

7. Dr. Laura Schlessenger is a radio talk show host/psychologist—"I Only Have Eyes for You"

8. The exercise machine made popular by Suzanne Somers' infomercials—"Phases"

9. Reference to Death/The Grim Reaper. This is a double: *The Seventh Seal*, which was spoofed in the movie *Bill and Ted's Bogus Journey*—"Killed by Death"

10. In the old *Invisible Man* movie the title character is "spotted" in a smoking jacket with a pipe that appears to float—"Killed by Death"

11. It's from *Jaws*, when shark expert Dreyfuss points out that boats don't usually leave teeth marks—"Go Fish"

12. *Jaws* again! This time it was the tag line for *Jaws 4*, where the shark seeks revenge in a human sort of way—"Anne"

13. *Jaws* (three times a fish guy). This classic line is uttered by Chief Brody (Roy Scheider) when he sees the shark for the first time—"Graduation Day"

14. *Mr. Belvedere* was a sitcom about a British butler in a very American household—"Dead Man's Party"

15. Weebles! Those egg-shaped children's toys were advertised with the tagline "Weebles wobble but they don't fall down"—"Dead Man's Party"

16. Mayberry is the quiet Southern town in the old *Andy Griffith Show*—"Faith, Hope and Trick"

17. Barbarino was Vinnie Barbarino on *Welcome Back, Kotter*, played by the charismatic John Travolta—"Band Candy"

18. Gene and Roger being Siskel and Ebert, the movie critics—"Some Assembly Required"

19. Okay, you're kidding, right? Yoda was Luke Skywalker's Jedi trainer in *The Empire Strikes Back*—"School Hard"

20. It's Power Rangers! (A joke based on the fact that Buffy's stunt double also plays the Pink Ranger)—"What's My Line"

21. An '80s singing family group known for their "leisure suit" look—"Welcome to the Hellmouth"

22. It's *murder* spelled backward, and it's from *The Shining*—"Puppet Show"

23. A reference to the villain in *The Usual Suspects*—"Puppet Show"

24. It's *Wizard of Oz,* when Dorothy wakes up and realizes that all her friends were cast in her dream—"Nightmares"

25. Soylent Green is a new food product made of ground humans according to the sci-fi flick of the same title—"Never Kill a Boy on the First Date"

Slay-O-Meter for Pop Goes the Culture

0–15   Jimmy Olson jokes are pretty much lost on you. Start working that TV remote.

16–30   If you don't mind a little Gene and Roger, you could use some more learning. Time to hit the video store.

31–50   You deserve an Oscar and an Emmy for outstanding achievement in useless knowledge.

5

Sophomore Year

> Welcome to Sunnydale. A clean slate, that's
> what you get here. We're not interested in what
> it says on a piece of paper even if it says—whoa.

"Welcome to the Hellmouth" and "The Harvest"

1. Upon arriving at Sunnydale High, Cordelia gives Buffy a coolness quiz. Can you pass it?

   a) Vamp nail polish
   b) James Spader
   c) Frappachinos
   d) John Tesh

2. Xander offers to pay Willow what sum of money for help with his math homework?

3. Upon meeting Buffy, Giles offers her a special book. What is it?

4. Two young ladies make fun of Buffy's unusual name. Who are these debs with no reason to talk?

5. Xander finds one of Buffy's stakes. What is his rational explanation for this?

6. What is Buffy's more plausible explanation?

7. Buffy tells Giles she had three fears upon starting school, and they didn't include vampires on campus. What were they?

8. What did Giles get as his freebie when he bought a Time Life series of books?

9. Name the vampire who is preparing for the rise of the Master.

10. What do the vampires call this day of celebration?

11. Angel gives Buffy a gift when they meet. What is it?

12. What is Buffy's short philosophy of life?

13. Name Xander's friend who makes even Xander look like a girl magnet.

14. Buffy has a surefire way of picking out a vampire in a crowd. What is it?

15. Why does Cordelia have to go call "everyone she's ever met"?

16. Who is Heinrich Joseph Nest?

17. Darla and the other vampire pick up some take-out food for the Master. Who or what is the meal?

18. How old is the Master?

19. The vampires know of another Slayer. When and where was she?

20. Willow uses her computer superpowers to access what?

21. What symbol designates the Vessel?

22. What is the Vessel?

23. How did the Master get trapped?

24. Who is the first to be fed upon as the Harvest begins?

25. What two common Bronze objects does Buffy use to slay?

"The Witch"

1. "This is madness! What can you have been thinking?" says Giles. What was Buffy thinking?

2. Who is the "stretchy" teen who goes up in flames?

3. Xander gives Buffy a present. What is it?

4. What award did Catherine Madison win?

5. What was her not-so-clever nickname?

6. Buffy thinks her mom had "Farrah hair" as a kid. Joyce corrects her. What kind of hair was it?

7. What is Cordelia doing when she loses her sight?

8. Who checked out the books *Witches, Historic Roots to Modern Practice,* and *The Pagan Rites?*

9. What ingredients are needed to test for a witch?

10. Name the science teacher who appears again in "Teacher's Pet."

11. Who is the cheer queen who loses her lips?

12. Buffy's next on the witch's hate list. What happens to her?

13. Catherine Madison can't control her daughter's witchcraft. Why?

14. What figural is Amy (or is it Catherine?) using to cast her spells?

15. Where does Catherine end up?

"Teacher's Pet"

1. Xander is slaying vampires, impressing Buffy, and man, what a guitar riff! What's up with that?

2. How *do* ants communicate?

3. Dr. Gregory was such a nice guy that it's a shame what happened to him. What *did* happen to him?

4. Angel arrives to warn Buffy about whom? Or what?

5. Name God's gift to the football team.

6. Who is Natalie French?

7. What is Cordy looking for in the cafeteria fridge?

8. What does she actually find?

9. "I'm an undead monster who can shave with my hand. How many things am I afraid of?"

10. Cordelia was so upset that she lost how much weight?

11. What is Ms. French's idea of lunch?

12. Name Giles's friend from Oxford and his area of expertise.

13. What do you call the chemical attractant that insects give off?

14. What does Ms. French want with Xander and Blayne?

15. Giles's friend was right about everything. Well, almost everything. What was he wrong about?

16. What is a Kleptes-Virgo?

17. What is the recommended method of slaying a she-mantis?

18. What is the significance of bat sonar?

19. Who leads Buffy to the she-mantis?

20. What is the last thing we see in the science closet?

"Never Kill a Boy on the First Date"

1. While professing "plunge and move on," Giles finds what on the ground?

2. This object is the symbol of what group?

3. Owen comes into the library looking for what?

4. Why does Giles want to declare a national holiday?

5. What prophecy predicts the coming?

6. When is the coming going to take place?

7. What does Giles say ninety percent of the vampire game is?

8. Buffy swears she won't wear her button that says what?

9. What cartoon character is on Xander's watch?

10. Buffy is torn between lipstick colors. What are her choices?

11. Name the militia man who dies in the van accident.

12. How does Giles evade the vampires at the funeral home?

13. What food product does Militia Guy seem to have a fondness for?

14. Where does Militia Guy end up?

15. Who is the Anointed One?

"The Pack"

1. Name the four kids who make up the Pack.

2. According to Willow, mating zebras look like what?

3. Name the nerd the Pack likes to pick on.

4. What does Xander say are the three things you need to start a school?

5. What is Xander's blood pressure?

6. Who or what is Herbert?

7. What happens to Herbert?

8. Explain why flunking math is bad.

9. What does the gang play in gym class on a rainy day?

10. Giles has a simple explanation for Xander's animalistic behavior. What is it?

11. According to Giles, what effect does testosterone have?

12. Why did Noah reject hyenas from the ark?

13. What tribe writes about animal possession?

14. What are the Primals?

15. Flutie is no more. Why?

16. Who's calling Willow?

17. What's up with the zookeeper?

18. What is necessary to perform the transformation?

19. Where does the zookeeper end up?

20. Xander and Giles share a secret. What is it?

"Angel"

1. What special event is happening at the Bronze?

2. What can you do to earn a free drink?

3. How does Buffy discover Angel's tattoo?

4. How does Buffy explain Angel's presence to her mom?

5. Buffy encounters three very strong vampires. What are they called?

6. To discourage visitors while training, Giles puts out a sign that reads what?

7. Buffy thinks Angel has read her diary. Who does she say that A stands for?

8. After a passionate kiss, Buffy discovers Angel's secret. What is it?

9. What is Darla's current outfit of choice?

10. Joyce becomes a vampire snack. Who does the nibbling?

11. The doctors say that Joyce was injured with what nasty kitchen implement?

12. Buffy tests her crossbow skills by shooting what?

13. Darla has a surprise for Buffy. What is it?

14. Darla is killed with an arrow. Who does the dirty deed?

15. What is the difference between the post-fumigation party and the pre-fumigation party?

"I Robot, You Jane"

1. The Slayerettes are involved in what mundane activity at the start of this episode?

2. What character is introduced in this episode?

3. Name the two computer geeks who have been seduced by the demon.

4. Name Willow's computer mate, and who is he really?

5. Computers are glitching. What strange report shows up on a student's laptop?

6. What doesn't appear on the nurse's computer?

7. Fritz is "jacked in." How does he mark himself?

8. What does CRD stand for?

9. Traditionally, how was the demon released from the book?

10. How did it happen in this case?

11. Ms. Calendar can help Giles put the demon back in the book. Why is she qualified to do so?

12. What magical rite must they perform?

13. Once the demon is sealed in his robot body, how is he killed?

14. When it's all over, Giles finds something of Calendar's. What is it?

15. She doesn't dangle it from her ear. So where does she dangle it?

"Puppet Show"

1. It's time for the Annual TalentLESS show, and Giles has the dubious honor of running things. Match the person to the talent. (List continues on next page.)

a) Cordelia   Magician
b) Lisa   Tuba
c) Marc   Dramatic scene
d) Morgan   Dancer

e) Sid	Singing "Greatest Love of All"
f) Emily	Juggling
g) Elliott	Controlling the ventriloquist
h) Buffy, Xander, and Willow	Ventriloquist

2. What cute little toy is on Willow's shirt?

3. Buffy says that dummies have given her the wig ever since she was little. What happened?

4. Emily gave of herself to the demon. What did she give?

5. There are three things Snyder will not tolerate. What are they?

6. How often does the demon need to seek out new organs?

7. "If I only had a brain." Whose does he have?

8. Why does Sid have it in for Buffy?

9. And what is his deal anyway?

10. What "actor" ritual does Giles inflict on the talent show cast?

11. Sid knew another Slayer. When and where?

12. The demon needs *another* brain. What was wrong with the first?

13. Whose brain is he after now, and how is he going to get it?

14. Who is the real demon?

15. Who kills the demon?

"Nightmares"

1. Everyone's nightmares are coming true. Match the nightmare to the dreamer:

a)	Spiders crawling out of a book	Giles
b)	Going to class wearing only underwear	Buffy
c)	Can't find the classroom	Xander
d)	Tacky clothes and frizzy hair	Willow
e)	Can't read	Cordelia
f)	Singing in front of an audience	Giles
g)	Clowns	Buffy
h)	Becoming a vampire	Xander
i)	Buffy's death	Wendell

2. As part of a nightmare, Buffy's father lowers what boom?

3. When Collin was mortal, what was he afraid of?

4. What kind of candy bar does Xander find on the floor of the school?

5. Why does Laura go into the school basement?

6. What does Ugly Man say before beating up Laura?

7. What poster can be seen when Laura is being attacked?

8. Name the little boy who is the cause of all the trouble.

9. What is done to make the nightmares stop?

10. Who is the Ugly Man?

"Out of Mind, Out of Sight"

1. It's time to vote—for what?

2. What is Cordy offering as a bribe?

3. Name the teacher who is helping Cordy with Shakespeare.

4. Marcie has three words for Cordy. What are they?

5. If Xander was invisible, what would he do with his power?

6. Harmony and Mitch—what is the common denominator?

7. What instrument does Marcie play?

8. What two books of Slayer prophecy were considered lost?

9. Angel says "not lost, just misplaced." Which book does he have?

10. What is the "kiss of death" when it comes to yearbook signing?

11. Giles has been looking for the mystical causes of invisibility. What should he have looked into?

12. Why does Marcie lure Giles, Xander, and Willow into the basement?

13. What is Marcie's plan for Cordelia?

14. Name the two FBI agents who show up just in time.

15. Where does Marcie end up?

"Prophecy Girl"

1. What California phenomenon begins the episode?

2. Giles finds a horrible prophecy in the *Codex*. What is it?

3. Xander has a much weightier problem on his mind. What is it?

4. Ms. Calendar has found three unusual events while surfing the Net. Name them.

5. Name the crazed monk who is sending out messages of doom.

6. What is the significance of Isaiah 11.6?

7. What gift does Joyce give Buffy?

8. How does Buffy stop Giles from going to fight the Master?

9. Who leads Buffy to the Master?

10. Where do they think the vampires are gathering?

11. Where is the Hellmouth actually opening?

12. Prophecies are tricky things. What's the part that Buffy missed?

13. Buffy dies, but only for a minute. How come?

14. Finish the quote: "I may be dead . . ."

15. What happens to the Master?

Answers to the Sophomore Year Quiz

"Welcome to the Hellmouth" and "The Harvest"

1. a) Over (so over)
  b) He *needs* to call me
  c) Trendy but tasty
  d) The devil

2. A shiny nickel

3. A very old and hefty volume with the word VAMPYR on the cover

4. Aphrodesia and Aura

5. She may be building a really little fence

6. It's for self-defense

7. "I was afraid I'd be behind in all my classes, that I wouldn't make any friends, that I'd have last month's hair"

8. A calendar (Jenny?)

9. Luke

10. The Harvest

11. A silver cross on a chain

12. "Life is short"

13. Jesse

14. She looks at their clothes ("deal with that outfit for a moment")

15. Buffy nearly staked her

16. The Master (Duh. Were you paying attention in chapter one?)

17. Jesse and Willow

18. 600

19. Madrid in 1843

20. The electrical tunnels under the city

21. A star with three points

22. He is one of the Master's minions; when he feeds, the Master grows stronger

23. He tried to open a dimensional porthole and got stuck

24. The bouncer at the Bronze

25. A pool cue and a drum cymbal

"The Witch"

1. She's trying out for the cheerleading squad

2. Amber Grove

3. An ID bracelet that says "Yours Always"

4. 1977–Tri-County Best Cheerleader

5. Catherine the Great

6. Gidget hair (Sally Field in a former life)

7. Driving in driver's ed class

8. Xander

9. Quicksilver, aqua fortis, and a bit of the witch's hair. Dump on witch and see if her skin turns blue. Oh, and you'll need some eye of newt.

10. Dr. Gregory

11. Lishanne

12. She's hit with a Bloodstone Vengeance Spell

13. 'Cause Catherine is really Amy and vice versa

14. Barbie dolls

15. Inside her prized trophy in the trophy case

"Teacher's Pet"

1. He's daydreaming in class

2. With touch and smell (and you didn't think TV was educational)

3. The Praying Mantis lady bit his head off

4. Fork Guy

5. Blayne Mall

6. She's the sub for Dr. Gregory. She's also the creature that ate his head.

7. Her medically prescribed lunch

8. Dr. Gregory minus his head

9. Not many, and not substitute teachers as a rule

10. Seven and a half ounces

11. Mayonnaise on white bread with crickets

12. Carlyle Ferris with an advanced degree in entomology and mythology (bugs and fairy tales)

13. A pheromone

14. She wants to mate with them

15. He wasn't right about his mother coming back as a Pekinese

16. A virgin thief

17. Slice and dice

18. Bats eat mantises, so their nervous systems go "kaplooie" when they hear the sound

19. Fork Guy
20. An egg sack

"Never Kill a Boy on the First Date"

1. A ring with a sun and three stars
2. The Order of Aurelius
3. A book of Emily Dickinson's poems
4. Because Buffy wants to check out a book
5. He will rise from the ashes of the five on the evening of the 1,000th day after the advent of Septus
6. Tonight
7. Waiting
8. I'm the Slayer—Ask me how.
9. Tweety
10. Red or peach
11. Andrew Borba—wanted for questioning about a double murder
12. He hides in one of the morgue drawers (already occupied!)
13. Pork and beans
14. In the cremation oven
15. Collin, the little boy who survived (sort of) the van crash

"The Pack"

1. Kyle, Rhonda, Tor, and Heidi

2. The Heimlich with stripes

3. Lance

4. Desks, some blackboards, and mean kids

5. 130 over 80

6. A pig masquerading as a razorback

7. He gets eaten by the Pack, including Xander

8. If you fail, you flunk out of school and end up being the guy at the pizza place who sweeps the floor and says, "Hey kids, where's the cool parties this weekend?"

9. Dodgeball

10. He' a 16-year-old boy

11. It turns all men into morons

12. Because he thought they were pure evil

13. The Masai of the Serengeti

14. A group of animal worshipers who pulled off trans-possession with animal spirits

15. He is eaten by the Pack, minus Xander

16. The Pack—it's a hyena habit to listen to a name and use it to lure a person to their death

17. He wants the trans-possession power for himself

18. A predatory act (like slitting Willow's throat)

19. He's tossed to the hyenas and eaten (we presume)

20. That Xander does remember everything said and did while possessed. "Shoot me, stuff me, mount me."

"Angel"

1. It's the annual fumigation party
2. Kill a roach and exchange it for a drink
3. He is hurt fighting vampires and she is bandaging his wound
4. She says he is tutoring her in history
5. The Three!
6. Closed for Filing—Please Come Back
7. Achmed, a charming foreign exchange student
8. He's a vampire
9. Catholic-school uniform
10. Darla, but everyone thinks it's Angel
11. A barbecue fork
12. A poster of a guy that reads "Smoking Sucks"
13. A set of Smith and Wesson revolvers
14. Angel
15. Much heartier cockroaches

"I Robot, You Jane"

1. They are scanning books into computers

2. Ms. Calendar

3. Dave and Fritz

4. Malcolm Black, or Moloch the Corruptor

5. "Nazi Germany was a model of a well-ordered society"

6. The fact that a particular student is allergic to penicillin

7. He cuts an M into his forearm with an X-Acto knife

8. Calax Research and Development

9. The book was read aloud

10. It was scanned (the computer "read" the book)

11. She's a technopagan

12. A circle of Kayless

13. Buffy short-circuits him

14. A corkscrew earring

15. Wouldn't you like to know???

"Puppet Show"

1. a) Cordy is singing "Greatest Love of All"

b) Lisa plays the tuba

c) Marc is the magician

d) Morgan is the ventriloquist (sort of)

e) Sid is controlling the ventriloquist

f) Emily is the dancer

g) Elliott is juggling

h) Buffy, Willow, and Xander are performing a dramatic scene

2. A rubber duckie

3. She saw a dummy and it gave her the wig ("there really wasn't a story there")

4. Her heart

5. "Students loitering on campus after school. Horrible murders with hearts being removed. And also smoking."

6. Every seven years

7. Morgan's

8. He thought she was the demon

9. He's a demon hunter cursed to live in the body of a dummy until he can kill all seven. He's got one to go.

10. The Power Circle

11. In Korea in the thirties

12. It was defective. Morgan had brain cancer.

13. Giles's brain, by cutting his head open with a guillotine during a magic trick

14. Marc

15. Sid

"Nightmares"

1. a) Wendell

    b) Xander
    c) Buffy
    d) Cordy
    e) Giles
    f) Willow
    g) Xander
    h) Buffy
    i) Giles

2. That he and Joyce's divorce was Buffy's fault

3. Monsters

4. Chocolate Hurricane

5. To smoke

6. "Lucky Nineteen"

7. Smoking Kills

8. Billy Palmer

9. They wake Billy by having him face the Ugly Man and unmask him

10. Billy's Kiddie League Coach

"Out of Mind, Out of Sight"

1. May Queen for the Spring Fling

2. Chocolates with a C on them

3. Mrs. Miller

4. Look, Listen, and Learn

5. He'd use it to protect the girls' locker room

6. Cordelia

7. A flute

8. *The Tiberius Manifesto* and the *Pergamum Codex*

9. The *Codex*

10. "Have a Nice Summer"

11. The Quantum mechanical. Physics!

12. She's going to kill them by filling the room with gas

13. She wants to cut up Cordelia's face

14. Agents Doyle and Manetti

15. At a special school for future political assassins

"Prophecy Girl"

1. An earthquake

2. Buffy will face the Master and she will die

3. He wants to ask Buffy to the dance

4. A cat gave birth to a litter of snakes, a family was swimming in a lake when it began to boil, and a boy was born with his eyes facing inward

5. Brother Luca

6. Luca's last message: "The wolf shall live with the lamb, the leopard shall lie down with the kid, the calf and the lion and the fatling together and a little child shall lead them."

7. A dress for the dance

8. She punches his lights out

9. Collin, the Anointed One

10. The Bronze

11. The library

12. She's the one who frees the Master. It's her blood that gives him the strength to escape.

13. She drowns, but Xander gives her CPR.

14. "But I'm still pretty. Which is more than I can say for you."

15. Buffy knocks him through the skylight, and he is impaled on a broken table in the library

Slay-O-Meter for Sophomore Year

1–90 D—You really need to study more! Time to review your vampire history before you become history yourself.

91–170 C—Not a bad report card. Three months of summer school and training with Giles should have you ready for anything the Hellmouth can throw at you.

171–260 B—You can skip summer school, but Giles is expecting you for prophecy study and hand-to-hand. Don't be late. You know how he feels about tardiness.

261–348 A—Wow! Straight A's. Forget summer school and tell Giles to give it a rest, you're off for a well-deserved vacation in Los Angeles.

6

Junior Year

It's incredible. One day the campus is completely bare, empty . . . the next, children are everywhere. Like locusts. Crawling around, mindlessly bent on feeding and mating, destroying everything in sight in their relentless, pointless desire to exist.

—*Principal Snyder*

Have you ever considered, given your abhorrence of children, that school principal is perhaps not your true vocation?

—*Giles*
"When She Was Bad"

"When She Was Bad"

1. Willow and Xander are passing time with a game of "movie quotes." Name the flicks:

　　a) "In the few hours that we had together, we loved a lifetime's worth."

b) "It's a madhouse. A madhouse."

c) "You're Amish, you won't fight back because you're Amish."

2. When playing Rock, Paper, Scissors, which one does Xander always choose?

3. Willow and Xander are attacked by vampires. Who arrives to save them?

4. How many vampires did Xander and Willow encounter over the summer?

5. According to Snyder, children are like what?

6. Where did Cordy spend her summer?

7. Jenny went to a festival. Name it.

8. Name the vampire who is assisting the Anointed One.

9. Xander and Willow swap snacks. Who gets what?

10. Giles attacks Buffy in the lounge. What's up with that?

11. To quote Willow, "What would somebody want with Master bones?"

12. In addition to the bones, what else do the vamps need for the ritual?

13. In what uncomfortable position does Buffy find Giles, Cordelia, Willow, and Jenny?

14. Ultimately, what happens to the Master's bones?

15. What does Cordy say is the worst part about her ordeal?

"Some Assembly Required"

1. Why is Giles talking to an empty chair?

2. The school is preparing for what event?

3. Chris has a buddy who likes to snap photos. What is his name?

4. What is Chris's science project? (Get this right and you get the Sunnydale Science Prize for your very own!)

5. What is Cordy's project?

6. Willow packs a special treat for "grave-digging night." What is it?

7. Name Chris's older brother.

8. How did his brother die?

9. What is Chris's mother watching on TV?

10. What do they find in Eric's locker?

11. Complete this quote: "Please call me Jenny. Ms. Calendar is . . ."

12. Where do Giles and Jenny go on their first date? (Did you say "date"?)

13. What is Chris trying to do for his brother?

14. Which Sunnydale student is chosen to contribute the head?

15. How is the "monster" destroyed?

"School Hard"

1. Who is Buffy tied with for Female Delinquent of the Year?

2. What happened to the horticulture teacher?

3. Snyder sentences the girls to do what?

4. What character(s) is (are) introduced in this episode?

5. How is the Welcome to Sunnydale sign destroyed?

6. The vampires are preparing for what holiday?

7. What happened to Spike at Woodstock?

8. Xander offers to help Buffy prepare for the vampires by doing what?

9. "La vache doit me touche de la jeudi." What did Buffy say in French?

10. What is Miss Edith's punishment for speaking out of turn?

11. Spike brings Dru a snack. What or who is it?

12. When the vampires attack, how is Xander able to escape?

13. Snyder covers up the vampire attack by claiming what?

14. Angel has a plan that involves Xander. What is it?

15. What is Spike's nickname for the Anointed One?

"Inca Mummy Girl"

1. Where do the Slayerettes go on their field trip?

2. What is it that keeps the mummy a mummy?

3. Who is the mummy's first victim?

4. What special event is going to take place at the Bronze?

5. Willow spots a clue that tells her that the mummy in the tomb isn't the real mummy. What is it?

6. Where is the mummy from, geographically speaking?

7. Where does the gang meet Ampata?

8. Name Cordelia's exchange student and the country he's from.

9. What snack food does Xander teach Ampata how to eat?

10. Xander's costume for the dance is from what country?

11. Willow is dressed in what sort of costume that catches Oz's eye?

12. What does Buffy find in Ampata's trunk, besides a lack of lipstick?

13. Why are Ampata's kisses deadly?

14. What is Giles's solution for stopping the mummy?

15. How does Buffy actually destroy Ampata?

"Reptile Boy"

1. Buffy and the gang are watching a movie made in what foreign language?

2. Name the fraternity that is at the center of this tale.

3. What college do they attend?

4. Name the cool college boy and his rather annoying friend.

5. Buffy finds a broken bracelet. What three letters are inscribed in the metal?

6. What is the missing letter?

7. According to Angel, why does the broken bracelet suggest foul play?

8. Giles is having a heavy-duty sword fight with whom?

9. Why does Cordy invite Buffy to the frat party?

10. Xander has to run the gauntlet at the frat house. How is he dressed?

11. How do the frat boys capture Buffy in their trap?

12. Willow admonishes Angel for not spending enough time with Buffy. Finish her tirade: "I mean you're gonna live forever . . ."

13. To what demon do the fraternity brothers pledge their allegiance?

14. The frat boys give the snake guy a yearly sacrifice. What do they get in return?

15. How is the snake killed?

"Halloween"

1. The vampires have a new weapon to aid in their fight against the Slayer. What is it?

2. Snyder is recruiting "volunteers" for what?

3. What do Buffy and Willow steal from Giles?

4. In order to keep Giles distracted, what little white lie does Buffy tell?

5. Time for trick or treat. What is everyone wearing?

　　a) Willow

　　b) Xander

c) Cordelia

d) Buffy

6. How does Buffy violate the "Guy Code"?

7. Ethan Rayne is running what kind of shop?

8. What is Ethan's curse upon the customers?

9. Ethan implores the statue of what god?

10. What does Mrs. Davis give as a "treat"?

11. Where did Cordelia buy her costume?

12. What is the significance of where she bought her costume?

13. What nickname does Ethan call Giles?

14. How does Giles break the spell?

15. What note does Ethan leave for Giles to find?

"Lie to Me"

1. What is Ford's full name?

2. How does Buffy know him?

3. Once heartbroken, Buffy sat in her room listening to what song?

4. What club have Ford and his friends formed?

5. What is the purpose of the club?

6. What is Diego's real name?

7. What character reappears in "Anne"?

8. Ford watches a movie on TV in the club. What is it, and who stars in it?

9. Jenny takes Giles on a surprise date. Where do they go?

10. Does Ford kill a vampire?

11. What does a vampire steal from the library?

12. What deal does Ford make with Spike?

13. Why does Ford want to be changed into a vampire?

14. How does Buffy outsmart Spike?

15. Buffy and Giles are waiting in the cemetery. Why?

"The Dark Age"

1. It's anywhere-but-here time. Name the fantasy:

    a) Buffy

    b) Willow

    c) Xander

2. Buffy calls it "Vampire meals-on-wheels." What is it?

3. Finish this quote from Giles in response to a question from Buffy: "Do you want me to answer that or . . ."

4. Giles lent Jenny his father's first edition book. Name the author of the volume.

5. What tattoo was all the rage with Giles and his friends?

6. Name the remaining members (or not so) of the group that Giles has listed in his notebook.

7. What, by profession, was Xander's infamous uncle?

8. Who does Buffy find lurking in the library stacks?

9. What happens to the bodies when Eyghon leaves them for another?

10. How does the demon choose its next host?

11. What photograph does Xander find among Giles's files?

12. According to Giles, this demon is different from most that Buffy has to face. Why?

13. Ethan has a solution to the problem—for him anyway. What does he do?

14. Who is the last human host for Eyghon?

15. How do they defeat the demon?

"What's My Line?" (Part 1 and Part 2)

1. What special activity week is the school involved in?

2. This involves taking what test?

3. Spike is trying to translate the volume that was stolen from Giles. Why?

4. Why is the text difficult to translate?

5. Where is the key hidden?

6. The key is actually what item?

7. Spike hires a group of assassins to take out the Slayer. Name the group.

8. How does Buffy kill the first assassin?

9. The second assassin is masquerading as what or whom?

10. Kendra comes to town. What's up with her?

11. Who is the real third assassin?

12. Name Kendra's Watcher.

13. What is the key to Dru's cure?

14. Oz has an interesting observation about animal crackers. What is it?

15. The church goes up in flames—but who emerges from the ashes?

"Ted"

1. If she were in charge, she would have the captain's hat. Who is she?

2. Does Ted have a last name?

3. What culinary creation requires the use of a cast-iron skillet?

4. He's not a chef, so what does Ted do for a living (and we use the term *living* loosely)?

5. How does Ted woo Willow?

6. How does Ted woo Xander?

7. It's time for a fun family outing. Where do they go?

8. If you look closely, you'll notice something is missing from Buffy's kitchen. What is it?

9. What does Buffy find on Ted's desk?

10. What does Ted find in Buffy's room?

11. The police have trouble believing that Ted hit Buffy. Why?

12. What is the secret ingredient in Ted's cookies?

13. Jenny and Giles take a stroll in the park. Why does Giles end up in the hospital?

14. What does Buffy use to short-circuit Ted?

15. Xander finds a surprise in Ted's closet. What is it?

"Bad Eggs"

1. Buffy and Joyce are doing something we've never seen them do before. What is it?

2. Buffy spots a vamp. How does she know he's undead?

3. Name the vampire and his brother.

4. Where are they from?

5. What is Xander and Cordy's favorite make-out spot?

6. Name the teen health teacher.

7. Why do the kids have eggs?

8. How did Buffy kill her gigapet?

9. What is Xander's secret to conscientious egg care?

10. That's no chicken inside the egg. What is it?

11. Cordy is carrying the latest style in backpacks. What is it?

12. How do the creatures take control of their hosts?

13. Who are the only two to avoid having their neurals "clamped"?

14. Momma Bezoar has a vampire snack. Who is it?

15. How does Giles explain away the circumstances after Buffy triumphs?

"Surprise"

1. In Buffy's dream, Willow is having coffee with an unusual friend. What's unusual?

2. What special occasion is rapidly approaching?

3. According to Cordelia, a date isn't a date unless what happens?

4. What's new with Spike?

5. A gypsy man comes to visit Jenny. Who is he?

6. For that matter, who is she?

7. What's going on at the Bronze?

8. Buffy wrestles a box away from Dalton the vampire. What's inside?

9. This box and a bunch of other boxes fit together to form what or whom?

10. Where does Angel go to begin his trip out of town?

11. Buffy and Angel end up wet. What happened?

12. What does Angel give Buffy for her birthday?

13. Dru has a rather appropriate song playing at her party. What is it?

14. One of the "good guys" is making a guest appearance in Buffy's nightmares. Who is it?

15. Buffy and Angel do something they'll regret . . .

"Innocence"

1. Angel's not the same in the morning. What's happened?

2. What is Jenny's secret mission in Sunnydale?

3. At the bus station, Xander got an offer he *could* refuse. What was it?

4. Dru is "naming all the stars." Why is that odd?

5. Willow makes a startling discovery. What is it?

6. According to Spike, this is a vampire's "raison d'etre."

7. How long has the Judge been "inactive"?

8. Buffy says that touching the Judge is akin to what?

9. The Judge tries to burn Angelus, but he can't. Why?

10. What do the books say about weapons and the Judge?

11. Who comes up with a plan to kill the Judge?

12. When sneaking onto the military base, Xander claims to be with what unit?

13. After killing the gypsy, Angelus leaves a message on the wall. What does it say?

14. Where does Oz suggest they go to find people lining up?

15. What does Buffy use to kill Big Blue?

"Phases"

1. Oz notices something strange in the school showcase. What is it?

2. What is Cordy's main concern after the werewolf attack?

3. What little kindness does Oz do for Willow in gym class?

4. Giles has a few props for today's lesson. What are they?

5. Name the werewolf hunter.

6. How many werewolves has he killed?

7. Why does he hunt werewolves?

8. According to the hunter, Buffy belongs to what type of rights group?

9. Who or what kills Teresa?

10. The werewolf attacks what two teen hangouts?

11. Xander says he's a werewolf expert. What makes him so qualified?

12. Who does Xander think is the "obvious" werewolf choice?

13. How does Buffy demonstrate her strength to the werewolf hunter?

14. Who is the werewolf?

15. What is his reaction when he discovers the problem?

"Bewitched, Bothered and Bewildered"

It's Valentine's day.

1. What does Xander give Cordy?

2. What does Angelus give Dru?

3. What does Angelus give Buffy, and what does the card say?

4. When are the girls going to stop teasing Xander about his dating Cordy?

5. Cordy chooses Valentine's Day to do what?

6. Amy's spell goes awry. What was it supposed to do?

7. What does it actually do?

8. What goddess does Amy appeal to?

9. What is the surprise that Xander finds in his bed?

10. What is Buffy's Valentine's outfit?

11. Amy also invokes the goddess Hecate for another spellcasting. Why?

12. Why isn't Xander safe at Buffy's house?

13. Xander is nearly killed by Angelus. Who saves him?

14. What tune is Oz singing when he searches for the Buffy rat?

15. How does Cordelia explain all the women ending up in Buffy's basement?

"Passion"

1. What artistic present is Angelus leaving for his "friends"?

2. Name Drusilla's new puppy.

3. Why does Cordy feel that she is in danger from Angelus?

4. What favor does Jenny ask of Willow?

5. Jenny makes a proclamation to Giles. What is it?

6. What happens to Willow's fish?

7. Why is Willow concerned about hanging crosses in her bedroom?

8. Jenny goes to the "boogedy-boogedy" store to buy what?

9. According to the clerk in the shop, this item is generally used as what?

10. But what is Jenny really planning on using it for?

11. What is Jenny translating when Angelus arrives?

12. What music is playing when Giles arrives home?

13. Giles finds a note that he thinks is from Jenny. What does it say?

14. What surprise does he find in his bed?

15. What happens to the disc with the translation?

["STOP"]

POP QUIZ

"Killed by Death"

1. Whom is Buffy battling in the graveyard?
2. Everyone brings gifts to the hospital. What did they each bring?

    a) Xander
    b) Willow
    c) Giles
    d) Cordelia

3. Buffy is afraid of hospitals. Why?
4. Buffy used to pretend she was a superhero. Name her.
5. Name Buffy's doctor.
6. Name the doctor who is trying to help the children.
7. What is Cordy's definition of "tact"?
8. What is the creature in the hospital called?
9. And what does his name mean?
10. Who helps Giles research the monster?
11. Why do the kids see the monster, when the grown-ups can't?
12. How does Buffy fix it so she can see the monster?

13. How does she kill the creature?

14. Ryan sends Buffy a present. What is it?

15. How does Buffy like her peanut butter sandwich?

"I Only Have Eyes for You"

1. What kind of dance figures in the plot?

2. A yearbook falls from Snyder's shelf. What year is it from?

3. What class is Willow teaching?

4. Willow gives Giles a present that had once belonged to Jenny. What is it?

5. Name the teacher who is haunting the school.

6. Name her student lover.

7. What surprise is waiting for Xander in his locker?

8. Giles thinks he knows the poltergeist. Who does he think it is?

9. What's a poltergeist?

10. What school employees are possessed by the two spirits?

11. Cafeteria food can be scary on a good day. What is today's special?

12. Willow does her Giles imitation and figures out how to trap the ghost. They need to create what magical shape?

13. What keeps Giles and the Slayerettes from entering the school?

14. Who are the last two people to be possessed by the spirits?

15. As an added bonus, we learn Spike's secret. What is it?

"Go Fish"

1. It's once, twice, three times a fish guy . . . name the swim team member who never made it off the beach.

2. What is the tattoo that identifies the remains of the swimmer?

3. The swimmers are tormenting one of the party goers. Who is it?

4. Gage is supposed to be making a pie chart. What is he actually doing?

5. What "friendly suggestion" does Snyder make regarding Willow's teaching position?

6. Buffy's in trouble with Snyder again. What did she do?

7. Name the coach of the swim team.

8. Where was Cameron Walker when his number was up?

9. Buffy was supposed to be protecting him, but who was it who ended up skinless in the locker room?

10. According to Buffy, what kind of creature eats humans whole except for the skin?

11. Is that Xander in the pool?

12. Who's the nurse who's helping turn these fish?

13. Who offers to "crack" the truth out of Jonathan?

14. Jonathan exacted his own kind of revenge on the swim team. What did he do?

15. How was the coach administering his special brew to the swimmers?

"Becoming" (Part 1 and Part 2)

1. What new character narrates this tale?

2. In keeping with the prior episode, what items does Xander use to reenact Buffy's fight?

3. What object is found while Willow is tutoring Buffy?

4. What does Spike identify as a "big rock"?

5. What will happen when the demon is awakened?

6. Buffy wants to try restoring Angel's soul. Who is adamantly against it?

7. Who is Mister Pointy?

8. Angelus needs an "old friend" to help him with the ritual. Who is it?

9. The vamps create quite a mess in the library. What happens to Xander, Willow, Kendra, and Giles?

10. Giles suggests that a certain mode of dress might help Angelus perform the ritual. What is it?

11. How is Giles convinced to reveal the missing piece of the ritual?

12. What is the secret to awakening the demon?

13. Buffy gets help from an unlikely source. Who is it?

14. What two characters are involved in a sword fight?

15. What ritual does Willow perform?

Answers to the Junior Year Quiz

"When She Was Bad"

1. a) *Terminator*
  b) *Planet of the Apes*
  c) *Witness*

2. Scissors

3. Buffy, back after being in L.A. for the summer

4. None

5. Locusts

6. Tuscany (she was hoping for St. Croix)

7. Burning Man in Black Rock

8. Absalom

9. Willow gets Xander's breakfast bar, he gets her apple

10. She is dreaming, and in the dream it isn't Giles at all but the Master in disguise

11. The vampires are planning to revive the Master

12. The people who were physically closest to the Master when he died—Giles, Willow, Cordy, and Jenny

13. They are hung upside down

14. Buffy grinds them into talcum powder with a sledgehammer

15. "None of that rust and blood and grime comes out. You can dry-clean until judgment day, you're living with those stains."

"Some Assembly Required"

1. He's practicing asking Jenny out on a date

2. A science fair

3. Eric

4. "Effects of Subviolet Light Spectrum Deprivation on the Development of Fruit Flies"

5. "The Tomato: Fruit or Vegetable?"

6. Little powdered donuts

7. Daryl Epps

8. He fell while mountain climbing

9. A video of Daryl playing football

10. A picture of a woman that is made from various photos torn from magazines

11. ". . . my father." (yes, you read that right)

12. The football game

13. Build a girlfriend for his brother, whom he brought back from the dead

14. Cordelia

15. He is killed in a fire

"School Hard"

1. Sheila Martini

2. Sheila stabbed her with a pair of pruning shears

3. They have to prepare the refreshments and decorate the lounge for Parent-Teacher Night

4. Spike and Drusilla

5. Spike drives his car through it

6. The Night of St. Vigeous

7. "Fed off a flower person and spent six hours watching my hand move."

8. Whittling stakes ("While I'm whittling, I plan to whistle a jaunty tune.")

9. "The cow should touch me from Thursday—and she said it wrong

10. "She will have no cakes today."

11. Sheila

12. Through an old entrance that was boarded up behind the stacks in the library (this is used a few more times after this episode)

13. It was a gang on PCP

14. He pretends to be "bad" using Xander as his victim

15. The Annoying One

"Inca Mummy Girl"

1. The Natural History Museum—presumably in Sunnydale

2. A seal (like a plate) with symbols on it

3. Rodney Munson—"God's gift to the bell curve"

4. A World Culture Dance

5. The mummy is wearing braces

6. The Sebancaya region of eastern Peru

7. The bus station

8. Sven from Sweden

9. A Twinkie, by shoving the whole thing into his mouth

10. Leone, which is Italy pretending to be Montana

11. An Eskimo

12. A bunch of boys' clothing and the mummy of the real Ampata

13. Because she sucks the life out of her victims so she can live on

14. They have to reassemble the broken seal

15. Buffy slams her into the stone pyramid, and she crumbles into dust

"Reptile Boy"

1. Hindi

2. Delta Zeta Kappa

3. Crestwood College

4. Tom Warner and Richard Anderson

5. E, N, T

6. K, to make KENT (for Kent Preparatory School)

7. It has blood on it. Angel can smell it.

8. No one—or should that be "himself"?

9. Richard told her she can't come unless she brings Buffy

10. Dressed as a girl with a wig and a huge bra

11. They drug her drink

12. "... You don't have time for a cup of coffee?"

13. Machida

14. They get to have a financially prosperous year

15. Buffy chops him in half

"Halloween"

1. A video camera

2. The students have to accompany a pack of kids as they trick or treat

3. One of the Watcher Diaries, so they can read up about Angel's life prior to him becoming a vamp

4. That Ms. Calendar said he was a babe

5. a) Willow is a ghost with a rocker babe costume on underneath

   b) Xander is a soldier

   c) Cordy is a cat

   d) Buffy is an 18th-century noblewoman

6. She saves Xander from being pummeled by Larry

7. A costume shop

8. People will become whatever they are costumed as

9. Janus

10. A toothbrush

11. Party Town

12. Her costume isn't cursed, so she doesn't change

13. Ripper

14. He smashes the statue of Janus

15. Be Seeing You

"Lie to Me"

1. Billy Fordham

2. They went to school together back in LA

3. "I Touch Myself"

4. The Sunset Club

5. They worship vampires, hoping to become one

6. Marvin

7. Chantarelle

8. *Dracula* with Jack Palance

9. To a monster truck rally

10. He pretends to but doesn't

11. One of Giles's books

12. If the vampires agree to change the group, Ford will deliver Buffy to Spike

13. He's dying from a brain tumor

14. She uses Dru as a hostage

15. They are waiting for Ford to rise from the grave

"The Dark Age"

1. a) An island beach, just before sunset, with Gavin Rossdale massaging her feet

    b) In Florence, Italy. Having ziti with John Cusack

    c) Amy Yip at the waterslide park

2. Blood supply delivery to the hospital

3. ". . . shall I just glare?"

4. Forrester

5. The Mark of Eyghon

6. Thomas Sutcliffe, Philip Henry, Deirdre Page, Ethan Rayne, and Rupert Giles

7. A taxidermist

8. Ethan Rayne

9. They liquefy

10. It jumps into the nearest dead or unconscious person

11. A photo of Giles as a punk rocker

12. Because he created it

13. He tattoos Buffy with the mark and burns his own off with acid

14. Jenny Calendar

15. Angel strangles "demon" Calendar until the demon jumps into his own "dead" body, where his own inner demon beats it to death

"What's My Line" (Part 1 and Part 2)

1. Career Week

2. Vocational Aptitude Test

3. It holds the key to curing Drusilla

4. They need a key to unlock the code

5. In the tomb of Josephus du Lac

6. A silver crucifix

7. The Order of Taraka

8. She slits his throat with the blade of her skate

9. Norman Pfister, with the Blush Beautiful Skin Care Company

10. She's a Vampire Slayer, called when Buffy died ("only a little")

11. The female police officer

12. Sam Zabuto

13. The blood of her sire—Angel

14. The monkey is the only animal that gets to wear clothes

15. A refreshed and revived Drusilla with Spike in her arms

"Ted"

1. Toni Tenille of the singing duo Captain and Tenille

2. Yep, it's Buchanan

3. Ted's mini-pizzas

4. He sells very expensive computer software

5. He gives her a few software upgrades

6. He gives him cookies and pizzas

7. To play miniature golf

8. A photo of her and her mom together

9. The photo of her and her mom, but it's been folded to show only Joyce

10. Her diary

11. Because she doesn't have any bruises

12. Dematorin, a tranquilizer

13. Jenny shoots him with the crossbow by accident

14. A metal nail file

15. Ted's first four wives

"Bad Eggs"

   1. Shopping at the mall
   2. He has no reflection in the mirror along the escalator
   3. Lyle and Tector Gorch (not the sharpest tool in the shed)
   4. Abeline, Texas
   5. The utility closet at school
   6. Mr. Whitmore
   7. It's an experiment in the responsibilities of parenting
   8. She sat on it and broke it
   9. A pot of scalding water and eight minutes
   10. A purple, slimy thingy, known as a baby Bezoar
   11. A backpack shaped like a stuffed bear
   12. They attach themselves to the host and take control of their motor functions through neural clamping
   13. Xander and Buffy
   14. Tector Gorch
   15. He says it was a gas leak

"Surprise"

   1. It's a monkey

2. Buffy's 17th birthday
3. The guy spends money
4. He's in a wheelchair
5. Her uncle Yanosh
6. She's Jana, of the Kalderash people
7. A surprise party for Buffy
8. An arm with a killer grip
9. The Judge
10. The docks
11. Buffy is thrown off the dock, and Angel jumps in to save her
12. A Claddagh ring
13. "Transylvanian Concubine"
14. Ms. Calendar
15. Buffy gives Angel one moment of true happiness

"Innocence"

1. He's had his soul taken away and he's evil once more
2. She was sent to watch Buffy and to make sure that she and Angel stayed apart
3. A 400-pound wino offered to wash his hair
4. Because she can't see the stars; she's looking at the ceiling. ("Also, it's day.")

5. She catches Xander and Cordy kissing

6. Killing people

7. 600 years

8. Getting a sudden, high fever

9. There is no humanity in Angelus

10. No weapon forged can stop him

11. Xander

12. The 33rd

13. "Was it good for you, too?"—and it's written in blood

14. To the movies at the mall

15. A rocket launcher

"Phases"

1. The cheerleading trophy that contains Amy's mom

2. That the werewolf wrecked her car

3. He tucks in the tag of her sweatshirt

4. A globe and a lamp, to show the effect of the moon on the Earth

5. Gib Cain

6. 11, to date. This one will make it a dozen

7. He sells their pelts in Sri Lanka

8. People for the Ethical Treatment of Werewolves

9. Angel kills her (but they think it was the werewolf)

10. The lover's lane and the Bronze

11. Because he remembers how it felt to be possessed by a hyena

12. Larry

13. She bends his rifle in half

14. Oz

15. "Whoa"

"Bewitched, Bothered and Bewildered"

1. A silver heart on a necklace

2. A human heart

3. A box of red roses with a card that says "Soon"

4. Never

5. Break up with Xander

6. Make Cordy fall desperately in love with Xander

7. Makes everyone *but* Cordy fall in love with Xander

8. Diana, goddess of love and the hunt

9. Willow!

10. Heels and a short raincoat with nothing underneath

11. To turn Buffy into a rat

12. Because Joyce is in love with him too

13. Drusilla

14. The theme to *Ben* (which was recorded by Michael Jackson for a movie about a boy and his rat)

15. She claims they were on a scavenger hunt

"Passion"

1. Sketches of them sleeping

2. Sunshine

3. Because she once invited him into her car, so now he can enter anytime

4. She wants Willow to take over her computer class so she can run an errand

5. That she's in love with him

6. She finds them in an envelope from Angelus

7. Because she's Jewish and her father wouldn't approve .

8. An Orb of Thesulah

9. A paperweight

10. It's a spirit ball used to capture and hold a person's soul

11. The Ritual of Restoration

12. "O Soave Fanciulla" from *La Bohème* by Puccini (get that right and you're an honorary Watcher)

13. "Upstairs"

14. Jenny—dead

15. It falls between the desk and the file cabinet, unseen

"Killed by Death"

1. Angelus

2. a) Balloons

  b) Homework

  c) Grapes

  d) Nothing ("I was out of the loop on gifts")

3. She saw her cousin die while in the hospital

4. Power Girl

5. Dr. Wilkinson

6. Dr. Stanley Backer

7. "Tact is just not saying true stuff."

8. Der Kindestod

9. Child Death

10. Cordy

11. He is visible only when you have a high fever

12. She drinks a dose of the virus to increase her fever

13. She snaps his neck

14. A drawing of Buffy as Power Girl standing over the broken body of the monster

15. Crunchy style with extra jelly.

"I Only Have Eyes for You"

1. A Sadie Hawkins Dance (girls traditionally invite the boys)

2. 1955

3. Ms. Calendar's computer class

4. A rose quartz necklace

5. Grace Newman

6. James Stanley

7. A decaying arm, which bursts out and grabs him

8. Jenny, of course, even though the parts don't fit

9. A disruptive spirit

10. The janitor

11. Snakes—lots of them

12. A Mangus Tripod

13. A swarm of black wasps

14. Buffy and Angel

15. He gets out of his wheelchair and stands. Spike can walk.

"Go Fish"

1. Dodd McAlvy
2. A cigar-chomping shark
3. Jonathan
4. Playing solitaire on the computer
5. She should give Gage a passing grade because he's on the swim team
6. She smashed Cameron's face into a steering wheel when he got fresh
7. Coach Marin
8. In the school cafeteria
9. Gage Patronzi
10. A demon with high cholesterol
11. No, it's Sean
12. Nurse Greenliegh
13. Willow
14. He peed in the pool
15. It was in the steam in the steam room

"Becoming" (Part 1 and Part 2)

1. Whistler
2. Fish sticks with a toothpick for a stake
3. Jenny's disc with the restoration spell on it
4. It's Acathla

5. Acathla will come forth and swallow the world, causing everyone to be sucked into hell

6. Xander, with Cordy chiming in on her own behalf

7. Kendra's favorite stake

8. Giles

9. Xander has his wrist broken. Willow is crushed beneath a bookcase. Kendra has her throat slit by Dru, and Giles is kidnapped.

10. "You must perform the ritual in a tutu."

11. When broken fingers don't help, Dru assumes the shape of Jenny and "vamps" (in the old fashioned sense) it out of Giles

12. Angel's blood

13. Spike, who agrees to help so he can get Dru back from Angelus

14. Buffy and Angelus

15. She restores Angel's soul

Slay-O-Meter for Junior Year

0–80   D—It was a tough year, losing Angel, seeing Giles deal with the loss of Jenny. All in all, you're not coping very well.

81–160   C—Okay, you learned some lessons. Don't go to frat parties. Don't trust old boyfriends, and next year it's "Xena" for Halloween. Take a deep breath and move on.

161–230 B—Think about it, Xander dated a mummy girl. Willow is dating a werewolf. So what if your boyfriend was an evil vamp. By Sunnydale standards you're doing all right.

231–310 A—You got off to a rocky start, but you caught Spike by the horns and saved the world. What more could a Slayer want?

7

Senior Year

I'm giddy. It's the freedom. As seniors, we can go off campus now for lunch. It's no longer cutting, it's legal. Heck, it's expected. But also a big step forward, a Senior Moment, one that has to be savored fully before, oooo! I can't!

> —Willow as she attempts to walk off campus during
> school hours for the first time
> "Faith, Hope and Trick"

Almost there, Buffy and the gang are rounding the corner, heading for that big moment in their lives: Graduation! But before they get there, Buffy's got a few more monsters to slay. Oh, yeah, and there's also that thing called the prom.

"Anne"

1. It's the start of a new school year. Where is Buffy?

2. The Scooby Gang is slaying. Who rises from the grave?

3. And why is he so spry?

4. Whom does Joyce blame for Buffy's troubles?

5. What is Buffy's new job?

6. What name is Buffy using as part of her disguise?

7. Buffy spots a familiar figure at the diner. Who is it and why is she familiar?

8. A young couple shows Buffy their tattoos. What are they?

9. Where did Cordy spend her summer?

10. The scary creature has a less than scary name. What does he call himself?

11. How does Buffy recognize the old man for what he really is?

12. Giles gets a tip that Buffy may be in what city?

13. What does the demon want with the runaways?

14. How is it that the kids age so quickly?

15. What *Buffy* crew member makes a cameo appearance as the "thug in the door"?

"Dead Man's Party"

1. Joyce has a new wall decoration. What is it and what country is it from?

2. What is Xander's slaying code name?

3. What piece of technical equipment is the slaying team using to keep in contact?

4. Xander thinks Buffy may have disappeared to what country?

5. Snyder thinks Buffy should seek employment at what fast food chain?

6. Joyce has a new friend. What is her name?

7. Where did they meet?

8. What appropriate book has Joyce been reading?

9. What is wrong with the cat Buffy finds in the basement?

10. The cat comes back. What's up with that?

11. According to Oz, name these types of parties:

    a) Brie and mellow song stylings

    b) Dip, less mellow song stylings, large amount of malt beverage

    c) Chock full of hoot and a little bit of nanny

12. Joyce's art object holds the power of what demon?

13. What is the power of the mask?

14. Giles shows off a talent that came from his days as a delinquent. What is it?

15. How does Buffy stop the creature?

"Faith, Hope and Trick"

1. Who is Hope in the title?

2. Where does Mr. Trick go for a late snack, and what does he order?

3. Mr. Trick is accompanied by one bad demon. Who is he?

4. Buffy's thinking "Kissing Toast," but what does the demon's name actually mean?

5. What's up with the vampire's hands?

6. Why is the vampire after Faith?

7. Buffy can return to school under three conditions. What are they?

8. While hunting a vampire in Missouri, Faith had to wrestle what kind of animal?

9. Where is Faith's Watcher?

10. According to Willow, Giles makes what sound when he's mad?

11. Giles needs Buffy's help with a spell. What spell is he working on, or is he?

12. What little nickname does Faith have for Buffy?

13. The Watcher's Council has a retreat (to which Giles isn't invited). Where is it held?

14. How is the vampire killed?

15. "Naked and shivering, virtually mad," who suddenly appears in the mansion?

"Beauty and the Beasts"

1. Willow is reading to wolfy-Oz. What is the book?

2. What happens to Xander while on "wolfy-Oz" duty?

3. Name the "happy on the surface" couple that is the center of this tale?

4. A boy was murdered in the woods. Name him.

5. Name the school counselor who becomes a chew toy.

6. Buffy runs into a "creature" in the woods. Who is it?

7. Willow keeps her morgue kit in what?

8. Giles is surprised to find Buffy sleeping with what two books?

9. Giles says there are two types of monsters. What are they?

10. Willow couldn't sleep, so she spent the morning where?

11. Buffy's lunch is made up entirely of this dessert.

12. How does Debbie explain her black eye?

13. What does Buffy tell her is the best way to deal with a black eye?

14. Which male beast is doing all the killing?

15. How is he destroyed?

"Homecoming"

1. A group of vamps, demons, and evildoers come to town for what event?

2. Name the evil participants (one point for each answer):

    a) Two terrorists
    b) The big-game hunter
    c) One spiney guy
    d) Two cowboy vampires

3. What is Cordy's campaign slogan?

4. Buffy brings Angel a snack. What is it?

5. Why does Cordy need an ice pack?

6. What two titles did Buffy hold at her old high school?

7. Why is Willow helping Cordy instead of Buffy?

8. What do Buffy and Cordy find in the limo?

9. Trick means to kill Buffy and Faith. Who does he get instead?

10. How does Mr. Trick explain the game to the girls?

11. How does Cordy rid herself of Lyle Gorch?

12. Who wins homecoming queen?

"Band Candy"

1. What kind of candy bars are the kids selling?

2. Despite the name, what is printed on the candy boxes?

3. An old "friend" of Giles comes back to wreak havoc. Who is it?

4. Name the elderly teacher who makes study hall a blast.

5. Giles has shed his tweed. What is he wearing instead?

6. Giles is rockin' to a tune from his past. Name the group.

7. Joyce is remembering a kinder, gentler band. What is it?

8. Willow's doctor and his friend are into a different tune. What is it?

9. Joyce takes a liking to a coat in a window because it reminds her of what singer?

10. Name the demon at the center of all the chaos, and what does his name mean?

11. What is the "tribute"?

12. How often must the demon be fed?

13. Where does the demon dwell?

14. Joyce has a useful "remembrance" from her frolic with Giles. What is it?

15. What was written on the school lockers?

"Revelations"

1. Name Faith's new Watcher.

2. What three books does the new Watcher expect to find in Giles's library?

3. The lady Watcher hits Giles with the ultimate insult. What is it?

4. A demon is on his way to the Hellmouth (surprise surprise). Name him.

5. The demon and the Slayerettes are looking for what?

6. Where is the item buried?

7. Buffy is training, but not with Giles. What is she learning, and from whom?

8. What startling news does Xander reveal to the gang?

9. Who are the Spartans?

10. Faith has plans for Angel. What are they?

11. Willow wants to tell Buffy a secret. What does she confess?

12. Giles is out cold again. Who's responsible this time?

13. What is required to destroy the demon prize?

14. What restores Willow's faith in Angel?

15. The council swears there was a memo. What was it about?

"Lovers Walk"

1. What kind of moron would want to come back to Sunnydale?

2. "This is a nightmare. My world is spinning!" What's wrong with Willow?

3. What does Cordy have in her locker that catches Xander's eye?

4. Oz gives Willow a "just because" present. What is it?

5. Giles is packing. Where is he going?

6. Spike has a rather rude awakening. What happens?

7. Skink root, essence of rose thorn, canary feathers—what is Willow brewing?

8. The last straw for Spike was when he found Dru with whom or what?

9. Why does Spike kidnap Willow?

10. Whom does he use as leverage to get her to cooperate?

11. Spike finds comfort pouring out his story to whose unlikely sympathetic ear?

12. How does Oz locate the missing Willow?

13. Oz and Cordy come to the rescue, but instead they get an eyeful of what?

14. Cordy has an accident. What happens to her?

15. Why does Spike change his mind about the spell?

"The Wish"

1. Buffy tries to make peace with Cordy, but Cordy ends up where?

2. There is a new girl in school. What is her name?

3. The demon's power is in wishing. Who made the wish and what was it?

4. When the world changes, Cordy's dressed all wrong. Why?

5. What are some of the signs that the world has changed?

6. In this reality Xander and Willow are what?

7. Whose favorite expression is "Bored now"?

8. Who are the "White Hats"?

9. Who or what is "The Puppy"?

10. What is different about Buffy in this reality?

11. What is Cordelia wearing that catches Giles's eye?

12. The demon is the patron saint of whom?

13. What does Giles have to do to "undo" what Cordy did?

14. What new plan does the Master have?

15. Buffy isn't as lucky in this reality. What happens to her?

"Amends"

1. What does Buffy see at the Christmas tree lot that helps her find the demons?

2. These demons have funky faces. What's wrong with them?

3. Whose life is shown in flashbacks?

4. What movie is Faith watching on TV?

5. Angel reluctantly seeks help from Giles, who greets him at the door with what?

6. What recurring character returns in the form of a demon haunting Angel?

7. Who are Margaret and Daniel?

8. The gang spends their Christmas vacation researching what?

9. What is unusual about Angel's and Buffy's dreams?

10. What is the First?

11. What are the High Priests of the First called?

12. What singer is heard when Oz visits Willow for their romantic evening?

13. The ghosts are forcing Angel to do what?

14. How does Angel plan on killing himself?

15. What miracle happens that saves Angel?

"Gingerbread"

1. Buffy is slaying in the park when who decides to join her?

2. What gruesome discovery do they make on the playground?

3. Giles thinks these are ritual murders. Why?

4. Name the male witch who is helping Willow and Amy.

5. Snyder is on a witch hunt; what does Xander have hidden in his locker?

6. What does Cordy have in her locker?

7. What does Willow have in her locker?

8. What is the odd-sounding acronym for the parents group?

9. What does the acronym stand for?

10. Mrs. Rosenberg can't remember Buffy's name. What does she call her?

11. Giles is on the Internet. According to Xander, what chat room is he visiting?

12. Name the two "dead" children (including their last name for the points).

13. What do the parents use for "witch-burning" kindling?

14. What happens to Amy?

15. How does Buffy vanquish the demon?

"Helpless"

1. Buffy isn't feeling herself. What's wrong?

2. What is Giles using to hypnotize Buffy?

3. Where is Buffy's dad taking her for her birthday?

4. What happened when Willow went to see Snoopy on Ice?

5. According to Oz, why is ice cool (and we're not talking temperature)?

6. Name the visiting member of the Watcher's Council.

7. Name the psycho vamp who comes with him.

8. What is the official name for the test Buffy must take?

9. Buffy is swatted down by a no-neck. Who rescues her?

10. What does Angel give Buffy for her birthday?

11. Where is Buffy's test to take place?

12. Who is kidnapped to ensure Buffy's co-operation?

13. What bit of modern technology does the vampire use to torment Buffy?

14. How does Buffy slay the bad vamp?

15. Why is Giles removed as Buffy's Watcher?

"The Zeppo"

1. What is the name of the bully in this episode?

2. How does Xander aggravate this ticking time bomb?

3. Name the group of female demons that is congregating in Sunnydale.

4. Xander is a key player in the Slayerettes. What is his job?

5. According to Xander, why is Oz cool?

6. Xander becomes "car guy" thanks to what kind of classic car?

7. Whom does the car belong to?

8. Who or what is Katie?

9. What kind of donut does Giles favor?

10. After being dead for eight months, what does Bob need to catch up on?

11. What is the criterion for joining Jack's gang?

12. Translate Jack-speak: "Bake a cake."

13. Giles is spouting Latin. Why?

14. Buffy's too busy to deal with Jack. Why?

15. What happens to Jack?

"Bad Girls"

1. The bad guys are into the funnies. Name the favorite comic strip of (give yourself one point for each right answer):

   a) The Mayor
   b) Mr. Trick
   c) The Deputy Mayor

2. Buffy's new Watcher arrives. What is his full name?

3. Name the vampires who carry two swords—one short, one long.

4. These vampires are the acolytes of whom?

5. What do these guys want?

6. Where will Buffy find it?

7. According to Wesley, a Slayer should remember three key words. What are they?

8. What are Faith's three words for a Slayer?

9. "Slayer is willful and insolent. Her abuse of the English language is such that I understand only every other sentence." What is Wesley reading?

10. Xander has developed a strange twitch whenever he hears what?

11. Faith makes a kill, but it's not a vamp. Who is it?

12. The mayor has four things to do on his To Do list. What are they?

13. How does Buffy kill the bad guy?

"Consequences"

1. Buffy's having a nightmare. What's it all about?

2. Joyce is watching the news. What channel is she watching?

3. What's the matter with Amy?

4. Who's got it bad for the new Watcher?

5. Wesley wants Faith and Buffy to investigate what?

6. Detective Paul Stein comes to talk to Buffy about the killing. Don't we know him from somewhere?

7. What is the mayor doing that usually lifts his spirits?

8. Faith decides to tell Giles the truth about the killing. What "truth" does she tell him?

9. Wesley tries to call the council, but he needs the code word. What is it?

10. Who saves Xander, and why does he need saving?

11. What is Wesley's solution to the problem of Faith?

12. What happens to his plan?

13. Where does Buffy find her?

14. Whom does Faith dust?

15. What important decision does Faith make that changes her future forever?

"Doppelgangland"

1. What magical feat is Willow practicing in the opening?

2. Name the jock whom Willow has to tutor.

3. There is a picture on Snyder's desk. What is it?

4. What is Giles eating in the library?

5. How does Faith define the obstacle field test?

6. What toy does the mayor give Faith, along with a new, fancy apartment?

7. What does Oz's shirt say?

8. What is Willow's first small step toward rebellion?

9. Anya and Willow perform a ritual that is supposed to do what?

10. What actually happens?

11. How old is Anya?

12. The gang is heading for the Bronze, but Willow runs back to the library. Why?

13. What is the signal that means Willow is in trouble in the Bronze?

14. What happens to the vamp Willow when she is sent back to her time?

15. After this glimpse of her bad-self, Willow decides she should stay home and do what?

"Enemies"

1. Buffy and Angel are on a date. Where are they?

2. What important package is the mayor expecting?

3. What happened to the last town to experience an Ascension?

4. Who is the demon who wants to sell the books?

5. How much money does he want Buffy to give him for the books?

6. The mayor offers Faith a drink. What is it?

7. Why is Giles hiding some of his books?

8. Xander comes up with the demon's address. How did he get it?

9. What happens to the demon?

10. What are Faith's plans for Angel?

11. What are Angel's plans for Buffy?

12. Who is the "best actor"?

13. Who is "second best"?

14. The Shaman owed Giles a favor. Why?

15. The mayor has two words to soothe Faith's blues. What are they?

"Earshot"

1. Buffy is fighting a demon, but what feature is missing from its face?

2. Name Sunnydale High's basketball star.

3. What is the first sign that Buffy has been infected by the creatures?

4. Using Giles-speak, the demon will infect Buffy with what?

5. Cordelia has knee marks on her back. Why?

6. Who is the first person Buffy "hears" and what is he thinking?

7. Giles thinks that Buffy would wear what kind of unusual footwear?

8. Principal Snyder has what song stuck in his head?

9. Why can't Buffy read Angel's thoughts?

10. What frightening thought does Buffy hear, loud and clear?

11. According to Giles, what will happen to Buffy if they can't stop the voices?

12. Who is really trying to kill the students?

13. What excuse do the Slayerettes use for questioning their suspects?

14. What ingredient is needed for Buffy's cure?

15. Why is the newspaper editor hiding from the Scooby Gang?

"Choices"

1. What university is Joyce proud that Buffy was accepted to?

2. Where is this university?

3. Willow was accepted to Giles's alma mater. Name it.

4. What book does Xander say will be his teacher?

5. What is the name of the mayor's special box?

6. What's in the box?

7. How does Buffy get the box?

8. How does Willow kill her vamp guard?

9. Buffy and the Mayor agree to an exchange—of what?

10. Name the mayor's deceased wife.

11. What does Snyder think is in the box?

12. Who saves Wesley's life?

13. What does Faith leave behind?

14. What does Snyder learn in this episode?

15. With so many colleges to choose from, where does Willow choose to go?

"The Prom"

1. Who is Xander's prom date?

2. Why did she pick him?

3. Xander's only other choice for a prom date is . . . ?

4. Name the dress shop where Cordy is working in secret.

5. Who buys Cordy's dress for her?

6. According to Giles, what is a hell hound's favorite snack?

7. Name the boy who is raising the hounds of hell.

8. What movies did he use to train his hounds to kill?

9. What does Giles offer Buffy when he learns that Angel is leaving?

10. According to Giles, Wesley has the emotional maturity of what?

11. Who wins the award for class clown?

12. What kind of award does Buffy win?

13. Who presents the award?

14. What common object was used to make the award?

15. Who is Buffy's prom date?

"Graduation" (Part 1 and Part 2)

1. Who is the professor Faith kills?

2. Why did she want him dead?

3. It's a tough day at school. What are the kids doing in Mr. Miller's class?

4. Who is the only person around to have lived through an Ascension?

5. During the Ascension, the person becomes the embodiment of what demon?

6. Angel is poisoned with a mystical compound whose name means what?

7. What is the only cure?

8. Buffy ends up in the emergency room. What happened to her?

9. The mayor has a special dinner on the eve of his Ascension. What is it?

10. If Buffy's plan sounds crazy, you should hear Oz's plan. What is it?

11. Thanks to a natural phenomenon, the vamps will be able to attend graduation. What is it?

12. Graduation day also happens to mark what historical event?

13. Principal Snyder joins the list of ex-principals. What happens to him?

14. After the carnage, Buffy's brain is stuck on what phrase?

15. What does it say on the cover of the Sunnydale High yearbook?

Answers to the Senior Year Quiz

"Anne"

1. Working as a waitress in some distant city
2. Andrew Hoelich

3. He was a member of the gymnastics team

4. Giles—much to his surprise

5. She's a waitress in a diner

6. Anne—if you got this one wrong you better quit now and go watch *Barney*!

7. She calls herself Lily, but Buffy knows her as Chantarelle from "Lie to Me"

8. They have two halves of a heart. His says Lily, hers says Rickie.

9. Club Med in Mexico

10. Ken

11. He has the tattoo that says Lily, identifying him as Rickie

12. Oakland

13. He brings them to his "hell" and makes them work until they die of old age

14. Time runs differently there than it does in the real world

15. *Buffy* stunt coordinator Jeff Pruitt (2 points for a right answer on this one)

"Dead Man's Party"

1. It's a mask from Nigeria

2. Nighthawk

3. A set of children's walkie-talkies

4. Belgium. Why wouldn't you go to Belgium?

5. Hot Dog on a Stick

6. Pat

7. At a book club

8. *Deep End of the Ocean*

9. It's dead

10. "Looks dead. Smells dead. But moving around. Interesting."

11. **a)** a gathering
   b) a shindig
   c) a hootenanny (okay, that one was a giveaway)

12. Ovu Mobani, or evil eye

13. It brings the dead back to life

14. He can hot-wire a car

15. She drives a spade into Pat's eyes while the creature lives inside her

"Faith, Hope and Trick"

1. Scott Hope, Buffy's new sort-of love

2. Happy Burger, a medium diet soda

3. Kakistos

4. "The worst of the worst"

5. They're cloven—as in hooves

6. She beat him in battle and destroyed one of his eyes

7. She has to pass a make-up test for every class she skipped, get a written recommendation from a faculty member (who is NOT a British librarian), and complete an interview with a school psychologist

8. An alligator

9. She's dead, killed by Taquitos—I mean Kakistos

10. A "weird 'cluck, cluck' sound with his tongue"

11. He says it's a spell to keep the vortex shut (it's just a ruse to get Buffy to talk about what really happened at the end of last season)

12. She calls her "B"

13. In the Cotswolds (England)

14. Buffy stakes him with a huge beam

15. It's Angel—he's back!

"Beauty and the Beasts"

1. *Call of the Wild* by Jack London

2. He falls asleep, possibly allowing wolfy-Oz to escape.

3. Pete and Debbie

4. Jeff Walken

5. Mr. Platt

6. A rather feral Angel

7. An old metal Scooby Doo lunch box

8. *Exploring Demon Dimensions* and *The Mystery of Acathla*

9. One wants to be redeemed, the other is void of humanity and can't respond to reason or love

10. At Mr. Donut

11. Jell-O

12. She says she hit her eye on a doorknob

13. Don't get hit

14. Pete doing his Jekyll and Hyde imitation

15. When Pete attacks Buffy, Angel snaps Pete's neck with a chain

"Homecoming"

1. Slayerfest '98

2. a) Hans and Frederick Gruenshtahler

   b) Frawley

   c) Kulak of the Miquot clan

   d) Lyle and Candy Gorch

3. "Get More with Cor"

4. A container of blood from the butcher shop, yum

5. To shrink her pores before having her picture taken

6. Prom Queen and Fiesta Queen

7. Because Cordy needs her help more than Buffy does

8. A note telling them to work out their problems and two corsages

9. Buffy and Cordelia

10. They watch a VCR tape on a TV in the woods

11. Still pretending to be a Slayer, Cordelia psyches him out with "I'm the queen, Buffy is just the runner-up"

12. It's a tie between Holly Charleston and Michelle Blake

"Band Candy"

1. Cocorific candy bars

2. Milkbar

3. Ethan Rayne

4. Mrs. Barton

5. Blue jeans and a white T-shirt

6. Cream

7. Seals and Croft

8. "Louie Louie"

9. Juice Newton

10. Lurconis; it means "glutton"

11. Newborn babies
12. Every thirty years (and this one's late)
13. In those dangerous Sunnydale sewers
14. A set of handcuffs
15. Kiss Rocks

"Revelations"

1. Gwendolyn Post
2. Hume's *Paranormal Encyclopedia, The Labyrinth Maps of Malta,* and Sir Robert Kane's *Twilight Compendium*
3. He's becoming too American
4. Lagos
5. The Glove of Myhnegon
6. In the Von Hauptman family crypt in Restfield Cemetery
7. Tai Chi from Angel
8. That Angel is alive
9. The fiercest warriors known to ancient Greece
10. She plans to slay him as a good Slayer should
11. That she opened her SAT test book five minutes early
12. Mrs. Post

13. Living flame

14. He saves her from Mrs. Post

15. That Mrs. Post was kicked out by the council two years ago for misuses of dark power

"Lovers Walk"

1. A lovesick vampire: Spike

2. She got a 740 verbal on her SAT's

3. Photos of the two of them

4. A Pez witch

5. A retreat in Breaker's Woods

6. His hand catches on fire when the sun comes up

7. A "de-lusting" spell

8. She was making out with a Chaos demon ("Have you ever *seen* a Chaos demon?")

9. He wants her to put a love spell on Dru

10. Xander

11. Joyce

12. He can smell her (can you say ewwww?)

13. Willow and Xander kissing

14. She falls through a broken step and is impaled on a steel rod

15. After a "decent spot of violence" he realizes that he should go back to Dru and torture her until she likes him again

"The Wish"

1. In a pile of garbage out behind the Bronze

2. Anya

3. Cordy wished that Buffy had never come to Sunnydale

4. She's wearing bright-colored "come bite me" clothes

5. Garlic hanging in the school, a curfew, very few students, everyone dressed in dark colors and with crosses, a monthly memorial service

6. Dead, or un-dead—as in vampires

7. Willow the vampire, aka Vamp Willow

8. Giles, Oz, Larry, and Nancy (and presumably others who are already dead)

9. Angel, a prisoner of the bad vamps

10. She's more of a street soldier, she's tougher, meaner, and she has a scar on her face

11. Anya's pendant

12. Scorned women

13. Destroy the demon's power center—that is, smash the pendant

14. He's automating blood removal

15. She is killed by the Master

"Amends"

1. A bunch of very dead trees
2. They have a runic symbol where their eyes should be
3. Angel's
4. *It's a Wonderful Life*
5. A crossbow, pointed directly at Angel's chest
6. Jenny Calendar
7. Two of Angel's victims from the past who are haunting his dreams
8. Why Angel has been brought back from the great beyond
9. They are sharing the same dreams
10. The first evil
11. Bringers or Harbingers
12. Barry White
13. Kill Buffy; to prevent it, he plans on killing himself
14. He waits outside for the sun to rise
15. It snows in Sunnydale, which blocks out the sun's rays

"Gingerbread"

1. Joyce
2. The bodies of two dead children

3. Because there was a symbol marking the hands of the children

4. Michael

5. *Playboy* magazines

6. $45 hair spray

7. Henbane, Hellibore, and Mandrake root

8. MOO

9. Mothers Opposed to the Occult

10. Bunny

11. The Frisky Watcher's Chat Room

12. Hans and Greta Strauss

13. Giles's occult books

14. She turns herself into a rat and escapes

15. She stakes him with the post she is tied to

"Helpless"

1. She's losing her strength and skills

2. A large blue grounding crystal

3. The ice show

4. She threw up on Woodstock

5. Because "it's water, but it's not"

6. Quentin Travers

7. Zackary Kralik

8. The Tento di Cruciamentum (if you got that one, you're an honorary Watcher!)

9. Cordelia!

10. A book of Browning's sonnets (and it looks like a first edition)

11. The old boarding house on Prescott Lane

12. Joyce

13. An instant camera. He covers the walls of one room with photos of Joyce.

14. She tricks him into drinking holy water

15. He failed the test when he told Buffy about it against the orders of the Council, and because he has a father-like relationship with Buffy, which compromises his work.

"The Zeppo"

1. Jack O'Toole

2. He misses a catch, allowing a football to fall in Jack's lunch

3. Sisterhood of the Jhe

4. Fetching the donuts

5. Because he's in a band

6. A blue 1957 Chevy Bel Aire Convertible

7. Xander's uncle Rory

8. Jack O'Toole's very large bowie knife

9. Jelly, but Buffy and Willow have eaten them all

10. Episodes of *Walker, Texas Ranger*

11. You have to die

12. Make a bomb

13. He's trying to raise the Spirit Guides

14. The Hellmouth is opening in the library

15. He is "eaten" by Oz the werewolf

"Bad Girls"

1. a) Family Circus (that PJ!)
   b) Marmaduke (nobody's tellin' Marmaduke what to do)
   c) Cathy

2. Wesley Wyndam-Pryce

3. El Eliminati

4. Balthazar

5. To recover an amulet that gave Balthazar strength

6. The Gleaves family crypt

7. Preparation, Preparation, Preparation (I know, one word three times)

8. Want, Take, Have

9. Giles's Watcher diary, chronicling his first days with Buffy

10. His eye twitches when he hears Faith's name

11. The deputy mayor, Allan Finch

12. Greet Scouts, Plumber Union Reschedule, Call Temp Agency, and Become Invincible

13. She electrocutes him

"Consequences"

1. She's drowning with the deputy mayor pulling her down while Faith holds her under the water

2. Channel 14

3. She's still a rat

4. Cordelia

5. The killing of the deputy mayor, "Natural or super, I want to know."

6. He's the same detective who came when Ted and Kendra were each killed

7. Using a paper shredder

8. That Buffy did it

9. "Monkey"

10. Angel—Xander is being strangled by Faith

11. He plans to return her to the council in England for trial and punishment

12. She escapes, leaving Wesley with a nasty bruise

13. At the docks about to hop a freighter

14. Mr. Trick

15. She gives her allegiance to the mayor

"Doppelgangland"

1. Floating a pencil

2. Percy West

3. A photo of a little girl (does Snyder have a spawn?)

4. A lollipop (watch closely and you'll spot him eating candy in several episodes)

5. "It's just like fun, only boring."

6. A PlayStation

7. "El Spado" with a bee

8. She eats her banana even though it's not lunchtime

9. Retrieve Anya's magic necklace, which Giles smashed in "The Wish"

10. It pulls Vampire Willow from the alternate world in "The Wish" into the gang's real world.

11. 1120 years old

12. To get the tranquilizer gun to use on the vamp Willow

13. Her screaming

14. She is staked by Wish-world Oz

15. Do homework, floss, and die a virgin

"Enemies"

1. At the movies
2. The Books of Ascension
3. The town of Sharpsville disappeared
4. Skyler
5. $5,000
6. Milk and alternately chocolate milk
7. They have magic secrets that he wants to keep away from Willow
8. He bribed Willy the Snitch
9. Faith kills him and takes the books
10. She's going to take his soul away again
11. He is going to torture her—or is he?
12. Angel
13. Faith
14. Giles introduced the Shaman to his wife
15. Miniature. Golf.

"Earshot"

1. Its mouth
2. Hogan Martin
3. Her hand itches
4. "An aspect of the demon"
5. From being part of a cheerleader pyramid

6. Xander. "I wonder if she [Cordy] and Wesley have kissed."

7. Cats strapped to her feet

8. "Walk Like an Egyptian"

9. "It's like the mirror. The thoughts are there, but they create no reflection in you."

10. "This time tomorrow, I kill you all."

11. She'll go insane

12. The lunch lady

13. It's a personality profile for the year-book

14. The heart of the demon

15. He wrote a bad review of "Dingos Ate My Baby"

"Choices"

1. Northwestern

2. Illinois

3. Oxford in England

4. *On the Road* by Kerouac

5. The Box of Garvok

6. Big, ugly, face-sucking spiders

7. Buffy and Angel break into the mayor's office and steal it

8. She uses a floating pencil as a stake

9. The box of Gavrok for Willow

10. Edna Mae
11. Drugs
12. Faith
13. The knife the mayor gave her
14. The mayor is more evil than he thought
15. UC Sunnydale

"The Prom"

1. Anya, the ex-demon
2. Xander isn't as obnoxious as the other boys, and he doesn't have a date
3. The sock puppet of love
4. April Fools
5. Xander
6. The brains of their foes
7. Tucker Wells
8. *Prom Night, Pump up the Volume, Prom Night IV, Pretty in Pink, The Club,* and *Carrie*
9. Ice cream
10. A blueberry scone
11. Jack Mayhew
12. Class Protector
13. Jonathan
14. An umbrella
15. Angel

"Graduation" (Part 1 and Part 2)

    1. Lester Worth

    2. He found the remains of an Ascension creature in a volcano, giving us a clue as to how to kill the thing

    3. Playing hangman

    4. The ex-demon girl, Anya

    5. Lohesh

    6. "Killer of the Dead"

    7. The blood of a Slayer

    8. She forced Angel to drink her blood in order to cure him

    9. The giant spiders from the box

    10. "We attack the mayor with hummus."

    11. A solar eclipse

    12. It's the 100th anniversary of the founding of Sunnydale

    13. The Mayor, in demon-snake form, eats him

    14. "Fire bad, tree pretty."

    15. "Sunnydale High '99, The Future Is Ours"

Slay-O-Meter for Senior Year

0–80 D—Senior year was full of hard lessons, but it's time you stopped brooding and got with the program. Angel's gone, but you still have a lot of living to do.

81–160 C—Well, you learned a few lessons: never hang a tribal mask in the bedroom; even Slayers must suffer the consequences of their actions; and there's nothing worse than a lovesick vampire.

161–240 B—That's a great report card considering all you had to deal with; the homecoming race, the prom, and Wesley! You done good.

241–319 A—Congratulations! You've survived high school!

8

Sunnydale's Most Wanted

Werewolves, zombies, succubi, incubi . . . everything you ever dreaded under your bed and told
yourself couldn't be by the light of day, they're
all real.

—*Giles on Sunnydale's monsters*
"Welcome to the Hellmouth"

What would a Hellmouth be without a wild
assortment of monsters creating mayhem to
lighten up an otherwise boring day? Match
these monsters to the form they take (list continues on next page):

Ms. French   Child killer
Eyghon   Mummy Girl
Ampata   Snake boy
The Judge   Demon who
                   inhabits the dead
                   or unconscious

Balthazar	Released from a book to the body of a robot
Der Kindestod	Praying mantis woman
Moloch the Corruptor	Prehistoric parasite
Machida	Big blue demon
Bezoar	Baby-eating snake
Lurconis	Jabba-ish creature with a perpetual itch

Answers to the Sunnydale's Most Wanted Quiz

Ms. French	Praying mantis woman
Eyghon	Demon who inhabits the dead or unconscious
Ampata	Mummy Girl
The Judge	Big blue demon
Balthazar	Jabba-ish creature with a perpetual itch
Der Kindestod	Child killer
Moloch the Corruptor	Released from a book to the body of a robot

Machida   Snake boy
Bezoar   Prehistoric parasite
Lurconis   Baby-eating snake

Slay-O-Meter for Sunnydale's Most Wanted

0–4 On par with Xander. "What? I can't have knowledge?"

5–8 On par with Willow. The only girl in school to have the city morgue in her computer bookmarks.

9–10 On par with Giles. "He's like Super Librarian. You forget, Willow, knowledge is power."

9

An Undead Kind of Love

"I'm naming all the stars."

—Drusilla

"Can't see the stars, love. That's the ceiling. Plus it's day."

—Spike
"Innocence"

Anthony and Cleopatra, step aside. Spike and Dru are taking over as the greatest lovers of all time. Okay, so they're a little freaky, and yes, they prefer shop-girls for their midnight snack, but do you know it all when it comes to Sunnydale's cruelest couple?

1. What episode introduced Spike and Dru?

2. In what city was Dru nearly killed by a mob?

3. What was the key to curing Dru of her illness?

4. What did Dru name the dog she found?

5. What was Spike's historical name?

6. Why do they call him Spike?

7. Whom does Spike have the distinction, and bragging rights, of killing in his past?

8. Where and when did Dru become a vampire?

9. What special event was going to happen the day she was changed?

10. Where did Spike and Dru set up house-keeping when they first came to Sunnydale?

11. On what street is the mansion that was their second home?

12. Why did they need a second home?

13. Name Dru's favorite doll.

14. Why does Angelus call Spike "Sit and Spin"?

15. What is unusual about the windows of Spike's car?

Answers to the An Undead Kind of Love Quiz

1. "School Hard"

2. Prague

3. The blood of her sire, Angel

4. Sunshine

5. William the Bloody

6. Because he used to torture his victims with railroad spikes

7. Two Slayers

8. London, 1860

9. She was about to take her vows to become a nun

10. The old factory

11. Crawford Street

12. Giles burnt the factory down when he came after Angel for killing Jenny

13. Miss Edith

14. Because Spike's in a wheelchair

15. They are blacked out except for a small patch in the windshield

Slay-O-Meter for An Undead Kind of Love

0–5 You're dinner. Next time don't accept rides from strangers (and these two are stranger than most).

6–11 Escaped by the skin of your teeth. Or maybe that should be the skin of their teeth. Better be more careful.

12–15 Are you sure you're on our side?

10

Band Class

"We have a marching jazz band?"

—*Buffy*

"Yeah, but you know, good jazz is improvisational. So we'd be marching off in all directions. Running into floats and stuff. Scary."

—*Oz*
"Beauty and the Beasts"

They say music hath charms to soothe the savage beast. Well, it may not soothe many of the monsters in Sunnydale, but the bands sure have a beat. Can you finish the names of these groups that have lent their vocal cords to Buffy?

1. Cibo ——————
2. —————— Monkey
3. Four —————— Mary
4. Act of ——————

5. Three Day _____
6. _____ Chain
7. Dashboard _____
8. Treble _____
9. Sarah _____
10. _____ Says

Second Chorus

1. What group plays for Dingoes Ate My Baby?

2. Name one of the composers who write Buffy's background music.

3. One of the cast members can be heard singing (okay humming) to one of the background tunes. Who is it?

4. Spike is belting out a tune at the end of "Lovers Walk." What is it?

5. In "Some Assembly Required," Eric likes to sing a certain song. Name it.

6. At the end of "The Dark Age," Giles jokingly makes mention of a group that suits his fancy. Who is it?

7. In "Witch," Buffy is singing a disco classic. Name it.

8. Xander is wallowing to what tune in "Prophecy Girl"?

9. What Barry White tune plays in the background for Willow and Oz's romantic evening?

10. What song is playing when Buffy and Angel dance at the prom?

Answers to the Band Class Quiz

   1. Matto (Cibo Matto)
   2. Sprung (Sprung Monkey)
   3. Star (Four Star Mary)
   4. Faith (Act of Faith)
   5. Wheely (Three Day Wheely)
   6. Velvet (Velvet Chain)
   7. Prophets (Dashboard Prophets)
   8. Charger (Treble Charger)
   9. McLachlan (Sarah McLachlan)
  10. Louis (Louis Says)

Answers to the Second Chorus Quiz

   1. Four Star Mary
   2. Christopher Beck
   3. Anthony S. Head can be heard humming in the "Jenny's dead" music from Passion
   4. A punked-up version of "My Way"
   5. "My Girl"
   6. The Bay City Rollers

7. "Macho Man" by the Village People
8. "I Fall to Pieces" by Patsy Cline
9. "Can't Get Enough of Your Love, Baby"
10. "Wild Horses" by The Sundays

Slay-O-Meter for Band Class

0–6   You can't carry a tune in a bucket. Better stick to sports.

7–15   Strictly a shower singer. Don't quit your day job.

16–20   Welcome to the band. The Dingoes could use a musical genius like you.

11

English 101

You forget, Willow. Knowledge is Power.

—*Xander on why Giles is Super Librarian*
"Never Kill a Boy on the First Date"

With all the slaying, Buffy barely has time to study. Give her a hand, crack open the dictionary, and see if you can figure out these Buffy episode titles from their dictionary definitions.

Example:
A small-scale figure.   Puppet
To present as a public spectacle.   Show

1. A group of persons, animals or things.
   A confection made of sugar.

2. The Marx Brother who wasn't funny.

3. Two people in love.
To move about in a visible form.

4. The award of an academic degree.
The time of light between one night and the next.

5. Some fitting together of manufacturer parts.
Necessary.

6. Any of a class of air-breathing vertebrates including alligators and others.
An immature male.

7. The act of communicating a divine truth.

8. Absence of light.
Era.

9. Mary Ann's shipwrecked movie star friend.
Grain product.

10. An annual football game that lots of alumni attend.

Answers to the English 101 Quiz

1. "Band Candy"
2. "The Zeppo"
3. "Lover's Walk"
4. "Graduation Day"
5. "Some Assembly Required"
6. "Reptile Boy"
7. "Revelations"
8. "The Dark Age"
9. "Gingerbread"
10. "Homecoming"

Slay-O-Meter for English 101

0–4 "I mean, in the real world, when am I ever gonna need to use chemistry, math, history or the English language?"

5–8 "To read English makes our speaking English good."

9–10 "I defined something? Accurately? Check me out. Guess I'm done with book learning."

12

Math 101

Xander: "Willow, could you help me with the math?"
Willow: "Which part?"
Xander: "The math."

—*"Welcome to the Hellmouth"*

Math takes a beating about as much as the vampires do in Sunnydale. Xander can't hack it, but Giles wished it could be "mathier"! Find the numerical answers to these questions, and earn yourself an A for effort.

1. What is Buffy's birthdate?
2. What was Buffy's grade point average when entering Sunnydale High?
3. How many people were in the group that raised Eyghon?

4. In what year did Angel become a vampire?

5. How many hell hounds were ready to snack on the prom guests?

6. According to Willow, Xander should change his phone number after dating Cordelia. What should his new number be?

7. What is Buffy's SAT score?

8. After a quiet summer, it took Giles how long before he had to consult his books?

9. How many natural elements are there?

10. What's the square root of 841?

Answers to the Math 101 Quiz

1. Either 10/24/80 or 5/6/79, neither of which corresponds with the birthday parties on the show

2. 2.8

3. 6

4. 1753

5. 4

6. 1–800-I'm-Dating-A-Skanky-Ho

7. 1430

8. 8 minutes and 33 seconds (Xander called ten minutes)

9. 103 (according to Willow in "Inca Mummy Girl")

10. 29 (again according to Willow, in "Puppet Show" this time)

Slay-O-Meter for Math 101

0–4 You're obviously waiting for the abacus to make a comeback.

5–8 "Sorry, I pretty much repress anything math related."

9–10 Like Giles, you're obviously bitter that there are only 12 grades.

13

Time of the Season

All right, I'll just drop in my time machine and go back to the twelfth century and ask the vampires to postpone their ancient prophecy for a few days while you take in dinner and a show.

—*Giles, on Buffy's date with Owen*
"Never Kill a Boy on the First Date"

From first season to last, there have been many memorable moments—shocking, sweet, scary, and silly. Do you remember in which episodes these events happened?

1. The death of Ms. Calendar.
2. Willow and Xander's first real kiss.
3. Oz sees Willow for the first time.
4. Joyce finds out that Buffy is the Slayer.
5. We meet Willow's mom.

6. Giles is removed from his position as Watcher.

7. Buffy marries Angel.

8. Oz learns he's a werewolf.

9. We meet Faith.

10. Giles and Jenny first kiss.

11. Xander and Cordy first kiss.

12. We meet Buffy's dad.

13. Giles laughs at one of Xander's jokes.

14. The Mutant Enemy logo guy in the end credits wears a hat.

15. Angel regains his soul.

Answers to the Time of the Season Quiz

1. "Passion"
2. "Homecoming"
3. "Inca Mummy Girl"
4. "Becoming, Part II"
5. "Gingerbread"
6. "Helpless"
7. "The Prom"
8. "Phases"
9. "Faith, Hope and Trick"
10. "The Dark Age"
11. "What's My Line, Part I"
12. "Nightmares"

13. "Phases"

14. "Graduation Day, Part II" (a graduation cap), and "Amends" (a Santa Claus hat)

15. "Becoming"

Slay-O-Meter for Time of the Season

0–5   Take two Buffy episodes and call me in the morning.

6–12   Mind like a steel trap. Unfortunately, it's rusted shut.

13–15   You've got the scoop on all the doings. May I suggest a job as the Sunnydale High Gossip reporter?

Slay-O-Meter

Time to add up your final score and see if you have what it takes to save the world from evil. Mark down your total from each chapter, then add them up!

Chapter One	"In the Beginning"	_____/25
Chapter Two	"Attendance"	_____/80
Chapter Three	"Knock, Knock; Who's There?"	_____/50
Chapter Four	"Pop Goes the Culture"	_____/50
Chapter Five	"Sophomore Year"	_____/348
Chapter Six	"Junior Year"	_____/310
Chapter Seven	"Senior Year"	_____/319
Chapter Eight	"Sunnydale's Most Wanted"	_____/10
Chapter Nine	"An Undead Kind of Love"	_____/15
Chapter Ten	"Band Class"	_____/20
Chapter Eleven	"English 101"	_____/10
Chapter Twelve	"Math 101"	_____/10
Chapter Thirteen	"Time of the Season"	_____/15
Total Score		_____/1262

Scoring

Time to check your answers and see where you land. Not everybody has what it takes to be a qualified Slayer, or even a Watcher for that matter (Wesley notwithstanding). Add up all your points, apply the bell curve, skew it in relation to your demographics, and average out your score. Awards will be handed out in a separate ceremony as soon as the high school is repaired. In the meantime, hang with your group:

0–250 You're a Cordette! You've earned the right to hang with Cordy and her pals. Proper attire a must, along with a charge card for Neiman Marcus and a love of cappuccino—extra foam.

251–500 You're a Slayerette! A score in this range gains you entrance to the Xander Brigade. You're right in the thick of things, but instead of a crossbow, a fresh box of donuts is your weapon. That's okay. What you lack in brains is made up for by being in the same vicinity as Willow.

501–760 You're in the Willow Study Group. Laptop required, and be careful with those spells! You could put someone's eye out! With a score like this you could go to any college of your choosing, but this being Sunnydale and all, we know where you'll go. . . .

761–1010 You're an honorary Watcher. Okay, so it's not an exciting life, but it has its perks. You get to hang with kids half your age and spend your nights with musty old books. Break out the tweed and bake up some scones, and when it comes to tea—no bags—only a ball will do!

1011–1262 You're ready to become the next Slayer! You've got what it takes—strength, skill, courage, and a bizarre sense of humor. You can take on the hounds of hell, just don't even try explaining that parking ticket to Mom. Hey, it's a dirty job but somebody has to do it. There's just one problem: Only when one Slayer dies is another called—so keep studying and stand by—Faith may be slipping, and your name is next on the list.

About the Author

Cynthia Boris has been hunting vampires since she was a little girl in New Jersey. She claims to have a few vamps among her close personal friends, but her son Josh is doubtful. In addition to writing for the *Official Buffy the Vampire Slayer Magazine,* Cynthia also writes a daily column on TV and movie collectibles for The CollectingChannel.com, and she is the author of *TV Toys and the Shows That Inspired Them.* Cynthia, her son, and husband live in southern California, not far from Buffy, and they have often walked the campus of Sunnydale High.

Bullying.
Threats.
Bullets.

Locker searches? Metal detectors?

Fight back without fists.

fight for your rights:
take a stand against violence

Everyone's got
his demons....

ANGEL™

If it takes an eternity,
he will make amends.

Original stories based on the
TV show created by Joss Whedon
& David Greenwalt

Available from Pocket Pulse
Published by Pocket Books

. . . A GIRL BORN
WITHOUT THE FEAR GENE

FEARLESS™

A NEW SERIES BY
FRANCINE PASCAL

A TITLE AVAILABLE EVERY MONTH

From Pocket Pulse
Published by Pocket Books